MULTIMEDIA SYSTEMS

MULTIMEDIA SYSTEMS

Rajneesh Agrawal
Bharat Bhushan Tiwari

EXCEL BOOKS

ISBN 81-7446-201-5

First Edition: New Delhi, 2000

Published by
EXCEL BOOKS
A-45, Naraina, Phase I,
New Delhi - 110 028

Printed at
EXCEL PRINTERS
NEW DELHI 110 028

Contents

Preface *vii*

1. Introduction 1
2. Music and Sound for Multimedia 19
3. Video 41
4. Images and Graphics 55
5. Compression 73
6. Storage Media 91
7. Multimedia Networking 113
8. Multimedia Platforms 145
9. Multimedia and Internet 161
10. Authoring System 181
11. Animation 197

Preface

This book provides an introduction as well as a reference to the Multimedia Systems, which provides the foundation and framework for many multimedia applications. This book will encourage students to learn about the concepts, tools and techniques of multimedia design. However, there is no prior computer experience required beyond the basic knowledge of computing. This book explains the basics of Multimedia and the Internet.

The reader of this book will be able to critically examine the various aspects of multimedia design, progression of computing technology and structure of the multimedia technology and develop an understanding of the theories and human-computer interface. Using creative approaches to multimedia computing, students will be expected to draw upon all their interests and abilities. Thus, students will be given the opportunity to explore a broad range of interactive media involving graphics, images, animation, video and sound.

Special areas of interest are Music and Sound, Video, Images, Compression and Storage Media. Special emphasis is given to Networking and Internet, keeping in view the requirement of technology for multimedia. The latest hardware and software developments are also described in chapters 8 and 11, namely Multimedia Platform and Authoring System.

A separate chapter on animation is also provided along with a chapter on Images. To provide a comprehensive presentation of the topics, this book is structured in various chapters to cover various aspects of multimedia.

In addition to the explanation of various topics, review exercises are also presented at the end of each chapter.

It has always been the purpose of this book to provide an introduction and overview that is valuable to the novice to find the bearings in the world of multimedia. For the benefit of readers and students who are new to multimedia, this book provides also some basic information which has been included in chapter 1. It is the main intention of the authors of this book to provide in-depth information on the most current technologies of multimedia systems available today and which are actually used. This material has been compiled as both an overview as well as a technical reference for advanced courses for students of DOEACC, All India Management Association (AIMA), Indira Gandhi National Open University (IGNOU) and various engineering and management institutions offering courses on multimedia.

CHAPTER I

Introduction

1. *Progression of Technology* 4
2. *Concept of Multimedia*.. 5
3. *Basic Terminology*... 7
4. *Hardware and Software Requirements*................ 8
5. *Applications*...11
6. *Conclusion*..17

CHAPTER 1

Introduction

There now exist a number of technologies that provide man with information such as computers, telecommunications and broadcasting, etc. However, until recently the human interfacing methods used to be restricted individually to characters alone, sound alone and so forth. With computers we can exchange information interactively on the basis of characters. Television offers moving images and sound but does not allow us to exchange information in interactive manner.

Each one of those technologies has so far built up its own technical concept within the limits of electronics, such as low CPU capacities. However, efforts are now being made to create human interfaces in more human friendly forms by overcoming those limitations with advancements in electronics. These are multimedia technologies with their origin in computer technologies, network technologies and broadcasting technologies, among others. All these multimedia technologies are oriented toward the same target and yet they vary in the manner they make progress, depending on where they had started.

Multimedia has the potential of forming the basis of a new civilisation which in turn has the potential to enhance the end user interface and to increase productivity. The multimedia revolution will likely accelerate and attract a large new population of computer end users as the cost of more powerful hardware and software continues to decline. When we compare the current scenario of Information Technology (IT) with what it was only in the nineties, revolutionary changes that have occurred can be felt. For example, by using e-mail on the Internet, one can communicate with people living all over the world easily and at a low cost. Also, through the Internet, we can access the large number of homepages over www (world wide web) that have been created. These homepages contain the multimedia documents. The www is a vast collection of interconnected documents through hyperlinks which span the world.

The development of multimedia and Internet has been so fast that we can easily predict that these technologies will change the lifestyles and cultures of many people. In fact, it will eventually form the basis of a new civilisation. This may be witnessed in freedom from constraints imposed by physical distance and other constraints of the real world using virtual reality.

Progression of Technology

Multimedia has not really been feasible until recently because computers have not been able to deliver an integrated package at an affordable price.

- In 1975, the first personal computers were marketed. Its features included a low processor power and black and green text-only screens. These were used in applications like accounting and inventory.
- By 1980, the personal computers had been augmented in technology by adding hard disk storage and simple graphics. These can be used in forecasting and statistics too.
- By 1987, the capabilities of personal computer had been increased manifolds. Now, these were capable of displaying

colour, providing more advanced graphics, sounds and animation. These were mainly employed in word processing and desktop publishing.

- Since 1995, we have the capability of integrating digital video, sounds, animation and text into one hardware and software package. There is an increasing emphasis on communications capabilities and sharing information over networks such as the Internet. These have now become popular in applications like simulations, Internet, communications and presentations.

Multimedia is made possible and affordable today because of increases in storage and speed and decreases in size and cost; this yields an increase in performance and availability.

Concept of Multimedia

The concept of multimedia has existed for many years. There is lot of confusion about what exactly is multimedia. A simple way of defining multimedia is that it denotes the combination of several media to transport information in several forms from one point to another. Technology has enabled us to so arrange these points that they could be situated within one room, within a city or country or located anywhere on the globe.

The transport media could be:

- copper or fibre
- radio or optical waves

The forms of information could be:

- text, audio or video (still or moving)

The terminal could be:

- fixed or mobile
- projection screen or TV tube
- notebook computer or PC

The terminal can use video clips, sound recordings, images, animation and text and can control external devices such as video recorder, video disc player, CD-ROM drive, synthesizer and video camera.

In a most general way, multimedia is defined as a system which exploits the computer to combine text, data, graphics, animation, voice and moving video into a single synchronised production or presentation. Under this definition, television is a multimedia device because it includes moving video, audio, text and animation in a single presentation system and uses computers in the process. The main focus in this definition is the computer's capability to exploit hardware and software to integrate different elements of the multimedia. These elements may be developed independently by various media sources into a multimedia user interface or presentation. Here, multimedia system may be grouped into two categories.

- **Linear.** If the end user receives a programme, which plays a sequence of sound, video and images without any control over the presentations' content, this is called linear or sometimes passive multimedia system. Videotape or a TV documentary may be cited as examples for this type of system.

- **Interactive.** In contrast to linear, if the programme lets the user control the sequence by selecting different options, it is called Interactive Multimedia (IMM) or non-linear multimedia. In other words, interactive multimedia systems achieve a higher level of information transfer because they provide customization that allows end users to receive data, information or knowledge and to actively participate in the process. IMM encompasses interactive marketing, interactive shopping, digital libraries, digital newsrooms, training-on-demand, video-on-demand (VOD), near VOD, electronic games, video mail and more.

The most common classifications of interactive multimedia are:

- A linear presentation is one in which the author decides the sequence and manner in which information is presented. The user controls only the pace.

- A programmed branching programme is one in which the user has some control over the sequence of presentation by selecting from a group of choices such as from a main menu. The author still maintains the control of deciding what to include in the choices available at any point in the programme.

Basic Terminology

- **Hypertext links.** A hypertext link is a special word, button or picture that, if you click on it, will move you to another page or display a document. It is often used to show more details about a particular topic. The special words with links to another page are normally described as hot words or hot links and are displayed in a different colour.
- **Pages.** Multimedia applications are normally made up of pages. Each page is really a screen full of information. If you are creating your own multimedia application, you can place text, buttons, images, sound or video clips on each page, then link the pages together so that a user can move through the 'book' (the name for a complete multimedia application with several pages).
- **Button.** A button is a little icon on screen that normally starts something if you click on it. Simple buttons are just square outlines, others have shading to make them look three dimensional. Buttons can start a video or sound clip or move to another page.
- **Audio.** It is the 'front end' of a multimedia system. It comprises an audio adapter, an audio input device such as a microphone, software to digitise the analog sound, amplifiers and speakers. You can also record and play back stereo CD quality sound or control electronic drum machines and synthesizer.
- **Video.** It is the other major 'front end'. Rapid advances in video digitalization technology have enabled video to be harnessed and deployed on the desktop. Real time video delivery, that is, delivering the presentation live, requires a high speed, high bandwidth network. A video clip is a sequence of images that are displayed rapidly to give the impression of movement. To

give smooth motion your PC needs to display over 25 frames per second - each frame is a separate image so even a short video clip takes up huge amount of space on your disk.

- **Animation.** It is yet another feature of multimedia capabilities. Two-dimensional (2-D) animation is the most common type today, such as cartoons. However, 3-D animation has mostly been confined to the engineering field like Computer Aided Design (CAD). As 3-D animation technology matures and becomes more competitive, this feature will also get into applications like on-line tutorials, simulations and virtual reality.

- **Virtual reality.** (VR) applications are programmes that could envelop a user within a 3-D simulated environment of sight, movement, sound and possibly touch in the future.

Hardware and Software Requirements

There are several important considerations when working with multimedia:

- Permanent storage is used to keep digitised information for future retrieval and use. Multimedia requires huge amount of storage during both the development and application stages. Many multimedia products require storage on a CD-ROM. Chapter 6 on Storage Media discusses this in detail.

- Bandwidth can be thought of as the pipe through which information must be pumped. The larger is the amount of data that needs to be delivered, the larger the pipe needs to be. This is currently the biggest limitation to delivering large amounts of digital video in multimedia. Optical fibre provides one of the largest pipes available.

- The processor speed is the ability of the computer to perform operations quickly. Because of the large amount of data required for sound and video, multimedia requires a fast processor speed. The new RISC-based processors provide speeds more then 400 MHz.

- The display depth is the ability of the display screen to project an accurate and rich image. Newer computers can display millions of colours and approach photorealistic images.

Hardware Requirements

The minimum recommended hardware requirement for multimedia is:

- Almost any Macintosh (they are built for multimedia)
- A PC with the following configuration:
  - 486/33 or higher processor
  - Sound board
  - 8 bit colour (256 colours)
  - Windows 3.1 or higher version
  - 350+ megabyte hard drive
  - double speed CD-ROM drive
- A laserdisc can be used to provide full-screen, real-time movies.

Hardware Standards and Platforms

Merging of sound and video elements with text, graphics and animation already used in desktop applications involves digitalization of analog signals operating on different standards and creating massive volumes of data. This requires compression algorithms to manage data storage and transfers fast enough to create smooth looking multimedia presentations. Joint Photographic Expert Group (JPEG), Motion Picture Expert Group (MPEG) and H.261 are major new compression standards for still image and moving video transmissions that are setting the stage for easy manipulation of all media elements and development of new products leading to integrated cost effective multimedia hardware platforms. These are discussed in detail in subsequent chapters. Chapter 5 on Compression explains different techniques employed in this process.

Several *de facto* multimedia hardware standards have emerged and have been promoted by hardware and software vendors eager to advance the multimedia business. These include the Multimedia PC (MPC) standard introduced by Microsoft, IBM's Ultimedia, Intel's Digital Video Interactive (DVI), Apple's Macintosh, Commodore's Amiga, Philips' Compact Disk-Interactive (CD-I) and NeXT Inc.'s NeXT and several engineering workstation platforms with Unix multiuser multimedia capabilities. Chapter 8 on Multimedia Platforms discusses various features of multimedia platforms in detail with specifications. Portable multimedia platforms are emerging rapidly with the advent of colour screen laptops and notebooks with CD-ROM devices and are seen as a major development in sales and marketing automation. Notebook computers are already outselling desktops in Japan.

Software Requirements

The software requirements for authoring multimedia may include Interactive authoring with animation, sound, video, graphical database for multimedia objects, screen captures, page layout for documentation, graphic creation and manipulation programme, presentations, graphic manipulation, hypermedia authoring programme, sound creation and editing programme, etc.

The success of multimedia depends on content and format of presentation much more than conventional information processing products. Therefore, many high level authoring systems have been developed to provide the software tools for developing multimedia applications with relative ease and without computer programming skills.

These authoring systems provide various facilities combining the functions of word processing and publishing, graphics and animation, special effects, audio and video support and interactive branching and system navigation. Many authoring systems include authoring languages to provide additional flexibility in linking multimedia systems with existing external sources of data and content materials and to facilitate networking applications.

Leading authoring systems offer versions operating under Windows operating system and many provide their own built-in GUIs. Some also include sophisticated iconic interfaces with decision tree flowcharting capabilities to facilitate multimedia application planning, documentation and maintenance. Various authoring system with their characteristics have been discussed in chapter 10 on Authoring Systems.

Applications

Digital video has a strong cross disciplinary nature, as demonstrated by the wide range of industries, including those involved with consumer electronics, telecom, computer, semiconductor, cable, broadcasting, medical imaging, photography, etc.

Digital video has many applications as follows:

- Distance learning which demands interactive TV using high capacity networks for satellites.
- Information (news) distribution which may be interactive, tailored to the customer's needs for both TV and newspapers.
- Entertainment will bring services like VOD and pay-per-view.
- Photographic application involving digitising film imagery, efficiently transmitting these data, editing and re-transforming into film, to accommodate both traditional and electronic cinema.
- Video on demand which requires improved computing and compression technology for delivering digital movies.
- Home shopping as it needs scanning of the shelves until one finds something he likes, then zooming into, rotate the object, try different colours and then buy it. For large purchases, for example, auto appliances, one could imagine a comparative shopping service with information on product specifications,

prices, delivery times and guarantee terms. There could be video presentation by manufacturers, independent product reviews, comments by satisfied and dissatisfied customers and discussion groups among consumers and producers. There could also be information to allow comparison of local distributors or service providers.

- Direct Broadcast Satellite (DBS) - Compressed digital video will allow DBS to compete with cable services. Assigning multiple channels to the bandwidth previously required, for one, reduces the cost and permits a sufficiently large number of channels.

- Video dial tone - An emerging contender in the market for consumer home video consumption is the phone company. The combination of the compressed digital video and emerging ADSL (Asynchronous Digital Subscriber Line) technology will allow the phone companies to offer 'video dial tone' over twisted pair copper cabling. Combined with a 'juke box' of movies, the phone company's switched service would allow it to offer true video-on-demand.

- Direct Audio Broadcast (DAB) - DAB will revolutionise the broadcast industry by transmitting CD quality music to home and car receivers. Europe and Canada have already conducted experiments involving the sending of compressed audio signals.

- Cable radio - MPEG audio compression will allow to transmit more channels of higher quality music through traditional cable lines and use fewer satellite transponders.

- CD-I video games and Karaoke - Compact Disc-Interactive (CD-I) from Philips is a product that needs little introduction. CD-ROM based technology is also finding its way into video games. The combination of compressed digital video and CD-ROM will allow games to feature full motion video. In Japan, similar technology is being used to create digital Karaoke machines, using CDs rather than laser discs.

- Video conferencing is another real time video application. A videoconference can be point to point between two locations and multipoint, which can include several conference sites, depending on the system's capabilities. In several situations, real time video delivery may not be necessary. In such cases, a store and forward technology is adopted, in which a user can access a library of video presentations from his multimedia computer. The bandwidth and network speed requirements are proportionately lower. Developments in CD-ROM technology, video discs and laser discs also have assisted video displays.

Educational Uses of Multimedia

Educational usage of multimedia is rapidly increasing. Its power to present information in ways not previously possible and its integration of resources allows for the creation of rich learning environments.

- In the past, a teacher or student had to consult many sources and use several media to access the needed information. By integrating media and utilising hypermedia we are able to create user controlled, information on-demand learning environments.

- Problems occur because of poorly designed programs, resistance to change within organisations and the lack of technology on which to run multimedia software.

- As technology costs come down, designers become better at producing programmes and users become more familiar with using multimedia, we will see a growing acceptance of it in educational settings.

Current uses of multimedia in education include:

- CBT (computer Based Training)

- Reference systems

- Simulations

- Virtual environments

- Edutainment is a hybrid of education and entertainment. It provides relatively equal emphasis on enjoyment and learning. Many products for home learning fall into this category.

Business uses of Multimedia

The term "business" used here means "productive activities at business corporations." Here some examples are being presented.

◆ **Information transmitting media used in business.**

In the productive activities at a business corporation, the introduction of computers is indispensable. In fact, computers ranging from small stand-alone word processors and personal computers to large in-house computing systems support the daily works. On the other hand, general information outside the organization can be acquired through computers by means of:

- **Personal computer communication.** This is a means that enables a multiplicity of personal computers to exchange electronic mails with each other, or to search for and retrieve databases by using telephone lines. The recent generalized use of PCs and the emergence of PC communication operators have prompted ordinary homes and offices to make use of this means.

- **Internet.** It provides services like www, news and e-mail, etc.

- **CATV.** Presently, the communication by CATV is done in one way – only allowing viewing images received from CATV companies. If the system can be provided with bi-directionality and the ability to control information received from CATV companies, the viewers will be able to select only the desired part of a program at desired time and the companies will be able to supply information that exactly suits the varying requests of the users.

Improvement in the work efficiency and the exploration of new business areas in productive activities at Business Corporations are some of the common issues for just about everybody engaged in the business. Sample applications of multimedia in business can be categorized in two categories:

◆ **Multimedia used individually**

- **Portable information communication devices.** This is a compact lightweight portable terminal device that allows data transmission and reception online. This is situated somewhere between an electronic agenda and a notebook type personal computer. It combines the communication functions, personal information management functions, documentation functions and others. Its intended users are marketing persons who mainly operate outside their offices. Other users are service engineers, medical staffs, etc.

- **Multimedia presentation.** This uses computers to combine information expressed in characters and illustrations with video and sound so that the information will be displayed more efficiently than conventional presentations based on OHP and slides.

- **Automatic translating telephone.** This is a telephone set that automatically performs simultaneous translation from a local language into foreign languages. Its success is largely dependent upon improvements in the voice recognition technique and automatic translation technique.

◆ **Multimedia used by multiple people (Group use)**

- **TV conference system.** This comprises TV cameras and TV monitors to televise the attendants located remotely from each other and thus enables them to hold conferences as if they were gathered in the same location. This is a good example of multimedia that has been used in practice since early times. Today, point to point TV conferences through ISDN or highspeed digital lines are most popular.

- **Multimedia conference system .** Evolution of multipoint conference method in the area of TV conference will eventually lead to structuring multimedia conference system that uses personal computers and workstations.

Conferences held this way will differ from TV conferences in the following aspects:

- While multimedia attendants share one single monitor in a TV conference, each person will use one terminal in a multimedia conference

- When the personal computer and workstations are equipped with the image communication function, e-mail function and highly functional software packages. These will not only allow the TV conference images to be switched or synthesized but also documents to be created, distributed, displayed, jointly edited and the meeting schedule coordinated, thus, allowing to process the entire flow of the conference electronically.

◆ **Remote education.** Remote education is a system that gives lessons by linking remote facilities to each other through communication channels and thus establishing communication between the lecturer and the students on a large size TV screen. It ought to represent the very first full-scale multimedia service implemented in the field of education and is presently drawing attention as a harbinger of the future style of education into next millennium.

◆ **Collaboration.** This means a form of work that is conducted for purposes of joint development and plan proposition by linking, through a network, the head office, plants, marketing branch offices and other facilities of a business corporation, separated from each other.

Especially, the form of work in which multiple workers access electronic drawings and data simultaneously for joint production is called CSCW (Computer Supported Cooperative Work).

◆ **Multimedia database system.** This is a kind of database that stores and unitarily manages all the data handled at a given business corporation, such as documents, ledgers, drawings, sound, static and moving images and so on. To enhance information processing functions of a business corporation , it is necessary to build up a comprehensive system that enables users to access multimedia databases from anywhere via network and to make effective use of the data retrieved in their offices.

Conclusion

For further evolution of multimedia, it is indispensable to provide an information communication infrastructure. Active movements are presently observed in connection with the construction of information communication infrastructure. Many countries are working on such plans like the National Information Infrastructure.

Review Questions

1. What do you understand by the progression of technology? Explain the same with respect to multimedia technology.

2. Give some applications of the multimedia.

3. What are the minimum requirements for hardware for multimedia system?

4. Give some educational applications of the multimedia.

5. Explain the business uses of multimedia.

6. How does multimedia conference system differ from TV conference system?

7. What is multimedia database system?

8. The phrases listed below refer to the construction of information communication in foreign countries. Mention the name of countries involved.

   i. RACE Project

   ii. IT2000 Plan

iii. Ultra High Speed Information Communication Construction Project

iv. NCIH

v. Telecom 2000 Project

CHAPTER II

Music and Sound for Multimedia

1. *Introduction* 21
2. *Audio Basic Concepts* 22
3. *Analog versus Digital* 25
4. *Digital Audio Basic Concepts* 29
5. *MIDI* 30
6. *MIDI Hardware* 33
7. *MIDI Messages* 35
8. *MIDI File* 37

CHAPTER 2

Music and Sound for Multimedia

Introduction

Sound is a physical phenomenon that stimulates the sense of hearing. It involves a vibrating object (sound source), a transmission medium (air), a receiver (ear) and a perceptor (brain). In humans, hearing takes place whenever vibrations of frequencies between about 20 hertz and 20,000 hertz reach the inner ear. Vibrations produced by sound source are responsible for repetitive, minute changes in air pressure and therefore causing pressure waves to travel away from the source in all directions. These vibrations can also travel through other materials such as wood, metal, water, etc. The speed of travel of these vibrations differs from material to material.

The repetitive minute changes in air pressure are called compressions and rarefactions. As pressure waves travel away from the sound source they become weaker as their energy is distributed over a wider and wider area.

When a wave travels, only the energy of wave motion is propagated through the medium; no portion of the medium itself actually moves very far. As a simple example, when the string of a guitar is played, a wave will travel down the string and produce sound. A wave can propagate transversely or longitudinally. A wave is called transverse wave when the wave moves transversely with respect to the direction of wave motion. The above example is a transverse wave motion. If the direction of the wave motion is parallel to wave movement, it is called longitudinal wave.

Audio Basic Concepts

The human ear listens to sound. The natural properties of the ear determine some essential conditions related to audio systems. Some of the important features are as follows:

- **Waveforms.** A waveform that repeats itself at regular intervals is called a periodic waveform. The unit of repetition in a periodic waveform is called a cycle. Some periodic waveforms such as sine wave, square wave, saw tooth wave, etc., have only one frequency component. Complex waveforms contain several frequencies simultaneously. A complex waveform can always be analysed as a sum of constituent sine wave.

Figure 2.1 Waveform in the form of sine wave

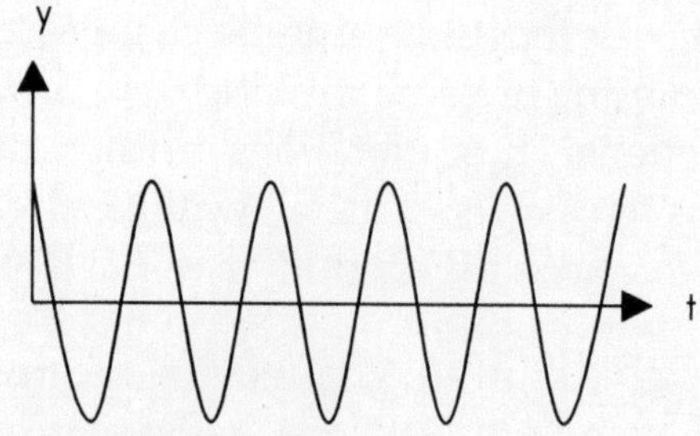

- **The attributes of sound.** Sound is described in terms of several characteristics: pitch, amplitude and quality.

- **Pitch.** Some objects like strings vibrate at discrete, well defined frequencies. A well defined frequency is discernable to humans as pitch. Human pitch perception lies between 20 and 20,000 cycles per second, or Hertz (Hz). In music, it is the highness or lowness of a musical tone as determined by the rapidity of the vibrations producing it.

- **Amplitude.** The amplitude of a sound wave is the degree of rarefaction and compression that accompanies the travelling wave. This is shown in the Figure 2.2 as the maximum change in amplitude. The perception of amplitude is called loudness. Loudness is usually measured in terms of decibels (abbreviated dB). The greater the amplitude of the wave the louder the sound is perceived. Decibels describe a logarithmic relationship between the amplitudes of two sounds where a doubling of loudness corresponds to an increase of 6 dB.

Figure 2.2 Amplitude

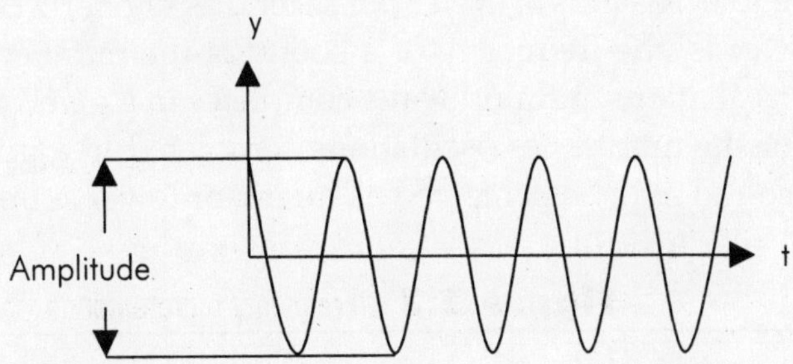

- **Dynamic Range.** The difference between the loudest and softest amplitudes that an audio system can produce is called its dynamic range. Good audio systems have a dynamic range of around 96 dB.

- **Noise.** Periodic waveforms that do not exhibit discernable regularity are called noise. The signal-to-noise ratio is the ratio in dB between the dynamic range and the ambient noise produced by the audio system itself. The higher the signal-to-noise number, the better the audio system.

- **Quality.** It is also called as timbre. If a tone identical in frequency and amplitude is played on a piano, a violin and a tuning fork all at the same volume, the sound produced by them will be different in quality. Of these three sources, the simplest tone is produced by the tuning fork. Differences in quality result from the fact that most sound sources vibrate at different frequencies (modes) simultaneously. The simultaneous frequencies contained in a waveform are called harmonics or partials. Harmonics in a periodic waveform are typically related by simple integer ratios to the main (lowest) frequency, called the fundamental. These harmonics are also known as overtones. The principle component of the note produced by the piano or violin also has a frequency of the notes produced by a tuning fork but these notes also contain components with frequencies that are exact multiples of the simplest tone which are harmonics/overtones. The exact intensity of these other components, which are called harmonics, determines the quality of the note.

◆ **Frequency.** Frequency refers to the speed of vibrations that causes a sound. How fast these vibrations occur is the frequency of sound which is measured in cycles per second or hertz (Hz) and thousands of cycles per second as kilohertz (kHz). In other words, the frequency of a sound is the number of cycles, or oscillations, a sound wave completes in a given time. Because of the number of oscillations completed in a given time, the sound may be perceived as higher or lower sounds.

Figure 2.3 Frequency representation

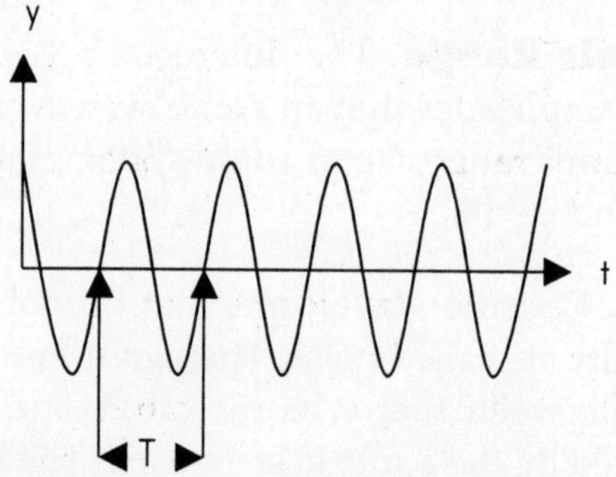

◆ **Intensity/Volume.** The distance at which a sound can be heard depends on its intensity, which is the average rate of flow of energy per unit area perpendicular to the direction of propagation. In the case of spherical waves spreading from a point source, the intensity varies inversely as the square of the distance provided that no loss of energy is due to viscosity, heat conduction, or other absorption effects.

Analog versus Digital

Communications can be classified in two categories:

- Analog
- Digital.

In the analog form of electronic communication, information is represented as a continuous electromagnetic wave form. Digital communication represents information in binary form through a series of discrete pulses.

Analog

Analog is best explained by the transmission signal such as sound or human speech over an electrified copper wire. In its native form, human speech is an oscillatory disturbance in the air as shown in Figure 2.1, 2.2 and 2.3, which varies in terms of its volume, or power (amplitude) and its pitch or tone (frequency). Analogous variations in electrical or radio waves are created in order to transmit the analog information signal for video or audio or both over a network from a transmitter (TV station or CATV source) to a receiver (TV set, computer connected with antenna). At the receiving end an approximation (analog) of the original information is presented.

Information which is analog in its native form (audio and image) can vary continuously in terms of intensity (volume or brightness) and frequency (tone or colour). Those variations in the native information stream are translated in an analog electrical network into variations in the amplitude and frequency of the carrier signal. In other words, the carrier signal is modulated (varied) in order to create an analog of the original information stream.

The electromagnetic sinusoidal wave form, or sine wave as shown in Figure 2.1, can be varied in amplitude at a fixed frequency, using Amplitude Modulation (AM). Alternatively, the frequency of the sine wave can be varied at constant amplitude, using Frequency Modulation (FM). Additionally, both frequency and amplitude can be modulated simultaneously.

Voice

A voice grade channel is approximately 4,000 Hz, or 4 kHz. Approximately 3.3 kHz (200 Hz to 3,500 Hz) is used for the voice signal itself. The remaining bandwidth is used for purposes of network signalling and control in order to maintain separation between information channels. While human speech transmission and reception encompasses a much wider range of frequencies, 3.3 kHz is considered to be quite satisfactory and is cost-effective. Band-limiting filters are used in carrier networks to constrain the amount of bandwidth provided for a voice application.

Video

A CATV video channel is approximately 6 MHz. Approximately 4.5 MHz is used for information transmission, while the balance is used for guard bands to separate the various adjacent channels using the common, analog coaxial cable system.

Digital

Computers are digital in nature. Computers process, store and communicate information in binary form, i.e., in the combination of 1s and 0s which has specific meaning in computer language. A binary digit (bit) is an individual 1 or 0. Multiple bit streams are used in a computer network.

Contemporary computer systems communicate in binary mode through variations in electrical voltage. Digital signalling, in an electrical network, involves a signal which varies in voltage to represent one of two discrete and well-defined states (Figure 2.4) such as either a positive (+) voltage and a null or zero (0) voltage, (unipolar) or a positive (+) or a negative (-) voltage (bipolar).

Figure 2.4 Binary representation forming digital signal

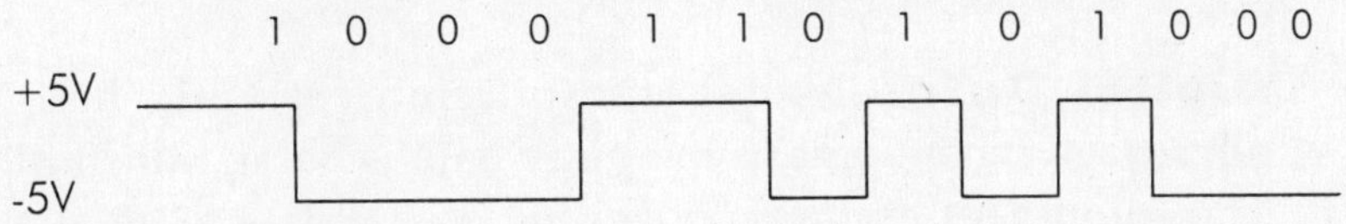

Although analog voice and video can be converted into digital and digital data can be converted to analog, even then each format has its own advantages.

Analog Advantages

Analog transmission offers advantages in the transmission of analog information. Additionally, it is more bandwidth-conservative and is widely available.

- **Cost effective.** Analog has an inherent advantage as voice, image and video are analog in nature. Therefore, the process of transmission of such information is relatively straightforward in an analog format, whereas conversion to a digital bit stream requires conversion equipment. Such equipment increases cost, makes susceptible for failure and can negatively affect the quality of the signal through the conversion process, itself.

- **Bandwidth.** A raw information stream consumes less bandwidth in analog form than in digital form. This is particularly evident in CATV transmission, where 50 or more analog channels are routinely provided over a single coaxial cable system. Without the application of compression techniques on the same cable system, only a few digital channels could be supported.

- **Presence.** Finally, analog transmission systems are already in place, worldwide. The interconnection of those systems is very common and all standards are well established. As the majority of network traffic is voice and as the vast majority of voice terminals are analog devices, therefore, voice communications depend largely on analog networks. Conversion to digital networks would require expensive, wholesale conversion of such terminal equipments.

Digital Advantages

- **Digital Data.** Digital transmission certainly has the advantage where binary computer data is being transmitted. The equipment requires converting digital data to an analog format and sending the digital bit streams over an analog network can be expensive, susceptible to failure and can create errors in the information.

- **Compression.** Digital data can be compressed relatively easily, thereby increasing the efficiency of transmission. As a result, substantial volumes of voice, data, video and image information can be transmitted using relatively little raw bandwidth.

- **Security.** Digital systems offer better security. While analog systems offer some measure of security through the scrambling, or intertwining of several frequencies, scrambling is fairly simple to defeat. Digital information, on the other hand, can be encrypted to create the appearance of a single, pseudo-random bit stream. Thereby, the true meaning of individual bits, sets of bits, or the total bit stream cannot be determined without having the key to unlock the encryption algorithm employed.

- **Quality.** Digital transmission offers improved error performance (quality) as compared to analog. This is due to the devices that boost the signal at periodic intervals in the transmission system in order to overcome the effects of attenuation. Additionally, digital networks deal more effectively with noise, which is always present in transmission networks.

- **Cost.** The cost of the computer components required in digital conversion and transmission has dropped considerably, while the ruggedness and reliability of those components has increased over the years.

- **Upgradability.** Since digital networks are comprised of computer (digital) components, they are relatively easy to upgrade. Such upgradation can increase bandwidth, improve error performance and enhance functionality. Some upgradation can be effected remotely over a network, eliminating the need to dispatch expensive technicians for that purpose.

- **Management.** Generally speaking, digital networks can be managed much more easily and effectively due to the fact that such networks consist of computerized components. Such components can sense their own level of performance, isolate and diagnose failures, initiate alarms, respond to queries and respond to commands to correct any failure. Further, the cost of enabling these components in such a manner continues to drop.

Digital Audio Basics

A sound vibration in the air is continuously changing and remains continuous even after getting converted into an electrical signal. This continuously varying sound is called an analog signal. Computer can only store numbers in binary format. Once the computer captures the sound, it does not have enough precision to store all the information about the sound to reproduce it perfectly. What the computer has stored is called a digital signal representation.

- **Sampling.** In the digital, numbers are used to represent a digital waveform. An audio signal is represented in digital memory with a binary code that stores a massive amount of numbers that are used to represent a signal. An ADC (Analog to Digital Converter) is a computer chip that is used to convert an analog signal into digital information. This process is called sampling and has changed the world of sound in a dramatic fashion. Once the signal is represented as binary numbers, it may be manipulated with processes like combining sounds, slicing, truncation, looping and reversing a sound and other digital signal processing. The signal is then converted back to an analog signal through a DAC (Digital to Analog Converter).

- **Sampling Rate.** The sampling rate determines the range of frequencies that can be represented in the digital recording. The more samples of a waveform are taken per second the closer the sampled result is to the original. A well known signal processing theorem (Nyquist Theorem) says that to accurately reproduce a signal, you have to sample at a rate at least twice the highest frequency component in the signal. As per audio specifications, CD sampling rate is of the order of 44.1 kHz, or 44,100 samples per second. Therefore, the CD sampling rate of 44.1 kHz will capture frequencies up to 22 kHz (a little past the 20 kHz specifications that most audio components try to achieve).

- **Sampling Resolution.** The size of the digital samples determines how accurately a signal can be sampled. 8-bit sampling is poor because only 2^8 (256) discrete levels of a waveform can be represented. 16-bit resolution can represent 65,536 different values so it is much better than 8-bit. Poor resolution ends up as noise in the audio output.

- **Digital Data Transmission.** A digital signal can be transmitted in two ways; parallel and serial. In parallel transmission each bit is transmitted along its own path. In serial transmission each bit is transmitted one after another along a single path. Parallel transmission is faster but also more expensive since multiple lines are provided for each bit. On the other hand, serial transmission is less expensive but also slower as it requires a fixed transmission speed and word size.

Musical Instrument and Digital Interface (MIDI)

The relationship between music and computers has become more and more important with the advancement in synthesizer technology. Synthesizers provide support to the musicians to create new and different sounds. This interface between musical instrument (Synthesizer) and computer is provided by a small piece of equipment that is connected to the serial port of the computer and allows the transmission of music signals. This is known as Musical Instrument Digital Interface (MIDI).

MIDI is not anything that the human ear would regard as music. That is why only electronic instruments listen to the MIDI signal. In other words, it is not an analog audio signal. The MIDI signal may be regarded as only control information. Most electronic instruments not only respond to MIDI data that they receive, they also automatically generate MIDI messages while the musician plays the instrument.

The Method of MIDI

MIDI is digital communications protocol that manufacturers of electronic music instruments have agreed upon. It is a set of specifications they use in building their instruments so that the instruments of different manufacturers can communicate musical information between one another without difficulty.

- A MIDI interface has hardware that involves a MIDI port and MIDI cables for establishing a physical connection in the same manner as two computers communicate via modems.

- The MIDI data format, that is digital, encodes the information travelling through the hardware. The encoding basically includes, besides the instrument specifications, when to start and stop playing a specific note, basic frequency, volume and modulation of note, if any. More recent applications include using the interface between computers and synthesizers to edit and store sound information for the synthesizer on the computer. These are grouped into MIDI messages. Each MIDI message communicates one musical event between machines.

- The MIDI data format is digital. The digital information is communicated in the form of bits. Through a combination of bits a vast amount of information can be transferred. Each MIDI command has a specific byte sequence. The first byte is the status byte, which tells the MIDI device what function to perform. Encoded in the status byte is the MIDI channel that is capable of communicating with other MIDI devices. The MIDI standard specifies 16 channels. Only the status byte has the MIDI channel number encoded. All other bytes are assumed to be on the channel indicated by the status byte until another status byte is received.

- Some of these functions indicated in the status byte are Note On, Note Off, System Exclusive (SysEx), Patch Change and so on. Depending on the status byte, a number of different byte patterns will follow. The Note On status byte tells the MIDI device to begin sounding a note. Two additional bytes are required, a pitch byte, which tells the MIDI device which note to play and a velocity byte, which tells the device how loud to play the note. Even though not all MIDI devices recognise the velocity byte, it is still required to complete the Note On transmission.

  The command to stop playing a note is not part of the Note On command; instead there is a separate Note Off command. This command also requires two additional bytes with the same functions as the Note On byte. Most people are confused at first by this approach to Note On and Note Off but on further thought they realize the necessity of the structure.

- To tune a MIDI device to one or more channels, the device must be set to one of the MIDI reception modes. There are four such modes:

  - Mode 1: Omni On/Poly
  - Mode 2: Omni On/Mono
  - Mode 3: Omni off/Poly
  - Mode 4: Omni off/ Mono

The first two modes describe how the MIDI device monitors the incoming MIDI channels. All the MIDI channels are monitored if Omni is enabled. In this mode, the MIDI device also responds to all channel messages. If Omni is not enabled, the MIDI device responds only to channel messages sent on the channels to which the device is set to receive.

Mode 3 and 4 describe how to play notes coming in over the MIDI cable. Several notes are played simultaneously in Poly mode. In Mono mode one note at a time is played.

MIDI Hardware

Ports

The MIDI interface is three 5 pin ports. These ports are labelled as IN, OUT and THRU. Through these ports, the computer can control the output of individual instruments. Of course a MIDI cable can be attached from the second instrument's MIDI OUT to a third instrument's MIDI IN and the second instrument will pass onto the third instrument those messages that the first instrument had sent. Now, all three instruments can play in unison. You could add a fourth, fifth, sixth, etc., instrument. We call this daisy-chaining of instruments.

- IN port – accepts data coming from an individual instrument/ source so that it may be reproduced by a sound generator.
- OUT port - The OUT port sends MIDI data out to the rest of the MIDI set up. These data result from activity of the synthesizer such as key presses, patch changes and so on.
- The THRU port also sends data out to the MIDI system, but not in the same manner as the OUT port. The data coming from the THRU port is an exact copy of the data received at the synthesizer's IN port. There is no change made to the data from the time it arrives at the IN port to the time it leaves the THRU port (which is a very small amount of time).

Cable

MIDI information is transmitted through a MIDI cable that has DIN-type male plug connectors with five pins to connect the synthesizer ports. Data is carried through the cable on pins one and three and pin two is shielded and connected to common. Pins four and five remain unused. MIDI cable is specially grounded and shielded to ensure efficient data transmission. This means that MIDI cable is a little more expensive than standard 5-conductor cable, but reliable data transmission is absolutely necessary for MIDI. The length of the cable is critical as well. An absolute maximum cable length of 50 feet is suggested. The entire length of a MIDI chain (discussed below) is unlimited, however, provided that none of the links are longer than 50 feet. The optimal maximum length for cable is about 20 feet and most commercially manufactured cables come in five to ten foot lengths.

The MIDI data is sent down the cable one bit at a time as a stream of information which is called a serial interface. MIDI manufacturers chose the serial interface because it is less expensive and more efficient than a parallel interface. The speed of a MIDI serial interface is 31,250 bits per second.

Computer Audio cards

Computer audio card that can record and playback digital audio has become a very supportive computer software tool. It is able to turn a computer into a device that can not only record and playback digital audio, but also present that data in a way that makes it easy for musicians to view and edit it. The data can be graphically displayed upon a computer monitor and can be manipulated. Furthermore, computer software can also perform its own manipulations of that data, yielding effects such as delay, transposition, chorus, compression, etc., sometimes even in real-time. In short, with good audio hardware and software, computers make very good digital audio workstations.

Synthesizer

The heart of any MIDI system is the MIDI synthesizer device. This looks like a piano keyboard. Most synthesizers have sound generators, microprocessors, keyboards, control panels, auxiliary controllers and memory as given below. There are many other MIDI devices that augment the standard synthesizer in a MIDI system like drum machines, master keyboard, guitar controllers and so on.

- Sound generators do the actual work of synthesizing sound and controlling the sound generators.
- Microprocessor is used to communicate with the keyboard and control panel; in other words, it sends and receives the MIDI messages.

- Keyboard provides direct control of the synthesizer.

- Control panel controls those functions that are not directly concerned with the keyboard. For example, panel controls include the slider that controls the overall volume of synthesizer, a button that turns the synthesizer on and off and a menu that calls up different patches for the sound generators to play.

- Auxiliary controllers provide more control over the notes played on the keyboard like pitch bend and modulation. Pitch bend controllers can bend pitch up and down to notes; modulation controllers can increase or decrease effects.

- Memory is used to store patches for the sound generators and settings on the control panel.

MIDI Messages

MIDI messages transmit information between MIDI devices and determine what kinds of musical events can be passed from device to device. A MIDI message is made up of an eight-bit status byte that is generally followed by one or two data bytes. MIDI messages are divided into two different types – channel messages and system messages.

- **Channel Messages** are those which apply to a specific channel and the channel number is included in the status byte for these messages. Channel messages may be further classified as being either channel voice messages, or mode messages.

- **Channel Voice Messages** carry musical performance data and these messages comprise most of the traffic in a typical MIDI data stream. The messages in this category are the keyboard action, controller action and control panel changes. They describe the music by defining pitch, amplitude, timbre, duration and other sound qualities. Examples of this are note on, note off, polyphonic key pressure, channel pressure, pitch bend change, programme change and the control change messages.

- **Channel Mode Messages** affect the way a receiving instrument will respond to the channel voice messages. They set the MIDI channel receiving modes for different MIDI devices, stop spurious notes from playing and affect local control of a device. Examples of such messages are local control, all notes off, omni mode off, etc.

- **System Messages** go to the entire MIDI system because such messages are not channel specific and no channel number is indicated in their status bytes. These are classified in three categories as system common messages, system real time messages, or system exclusive messages.

- **System Common Messages** are intended for all receivers in the system. These are commands that prepare sequencers and synthesizers to play a song. The various messages enable selection of a song, find a common starting place in the song and tune all the synthesizers if need be. Examples of such messages are MTC (MIDI Time Code), quarter frame (information used for synchronisation of MIDI equipment and other equipment), song select, song position pointer, tune request and End Of Exclusive (EOX).

- **System Real Time Messages** are used for synchronisation between clock-based MIDI components/equipment within a system, such as sequencers and drum machines. Most of the system real time messages are normally ignored by keyboard instruments and synthesizers. To help ensure accurate timing, system real time messages are given priority over other messages and these very short, simple and single-byte messages may occur anywhere in the data stream (a real time message may appear between the status byte and data byte of some other MIDI message). The system real time messages are the timing clock, start, continue, stop, active sensing and the system reset message.

- **System Exclusive Messages** include a manufacturer's identification (ID) code and are used to transfer any number of data bytes in a format specified by the referenced manufacturer. The manufacturers ID is followed by any number of data bytes and the data transmission is terminated with the EOX message. Manufacturers are required to publish the details of their System

Exclusive data formats and other manufacturers may freely utilise these formats provided that they do not alter or utilise the format in a way which conflicts with the original manufacturers specifications. Certain system exclusive ID numbers are reserved for special protocols. Among these are the MIDI sample dump standard, which is a system exclusive data format defined in the MIDI specification for the transmission of sample data between MIDI devices as well as MIDI show control and MIDI machine control.

MIDI File

A MIDI file is a data file that contains musical information. Specifically, a MIDI file stores MIDI data in the form of commands that musical instruments transmit between each other to control playing notes and adjusting an instrument's sound, etc. MIDI is binary data and a MIDI file is, therefore, a binary file. You can't load a MIDI file into a text editor and view it.

The MIDI file format was devised to be able to store any kind of MIDI messages, including system exclusive messages, alongwith a timestamp for each MIDI message. A timestamp is simply the time when the message was generated. Using the timestamps, a sequencer can playback all of the MIDI messages within the MIDI file at the same relative times as when the messages were originally generated. In other words, sequencers can play back the entire note messages and other MIDI messages with the original musical rhythms. A MIDI file can also store other information relating to a musical performance, such as tempo, key signature and time signature. A MIDI file is therefore a generic, standardised file format designed to store musical performances and is used by many sequencers. A MIDI file even has provisions for storing the names of tracks in a sequencer and other sequencer settings.

MIDI files are not specific to any particular computer platform or product. There are three different type MIDI files or formats.

- Type 0 files contain only one track and entire MIDI messages are placed in that one track, even if it represents many musical parts upon different MIDI channels.

- Type 1 files separate each musical part upon its own track. Both Type 0 and 1 store one musical performance.
- Type 2 files which are extremely rare, are akin to a collection of Type 0 files all crammed into one MIDI file. Type 2 is used to store a collection of songs or patterns, for example, numerous drumbeats.

MIDI File and Wave File

A MIDI file stores MIDI messages which are commands that tell a musical device what to do in order to make music. For example, there is a MIDI message that tells a device to play a particular note. There is another MIDI message that tells a device to change its current sound to a particular patch or instrument. The MIDI file also stores timestamps and other information that a sequencer needs to play some musical performance by transmitting all of the MIDI messages in the file to all MIDI devices.

A wave file stores a digital audio waveform. This data must be played back upon a device with a Digital to Analog Converter (DAC). There are no timestamps or other information concerning musical rhythms or tempo stored in a wave file but only digital audio data.

The only way to record and store a musical performance within a wave file is to digitise the audio output of all instruments while they play that performance. The result will be a typically large wave file that represents the digitised sound of all instruments playing the musical piece in real time. The act of doing such is often referred to as hard disk recording because the wave data usually has to be recorded directly to a large hard drive while the DAC digitises the performance.

A MIDI file allows easy editing of the individual musical parts because each part is usually assigned to its own MIDI channel and it is easy to separate that part's MIDI data from the other parts' MIDI data, based upon the MIDI channel in each MIDI message. On the other hand, the digital audio data of one instrument cannot be separated from the digital audio data of another instrument if the two were digitised simultaneously into one wave file. For editing of individual musical parts, each part should be digitised and stored in its own wave file. Due to the difficulties in separating musical parts from a wave file, a conversion from wave format to MIDI format is not too feasible, although the reverse is not a problem.

One benefit of a wave file is that its sound is not usually dependent upon the playback device. A wave file should sound the same upon different equipment with reasonably similar specifications. On the other hand, a MIDI file can sound considerably different upon different MIDI gear. This is because the MIDI file does not dictate what means an instrument uses to produce its sound.

Review Questions

1. What is dynamic range?
2. What is pitch of sound?
3. Define digital and analog signals.
4. Why have digital signals gained wide acceptability over analog signals?
5. What are the different types of MIDI files?
6. How can MIDI file and wave file be differentiated?
7. What are the MIDI messages? Explain.
8. What are the basic hardware for MIDI?

CHAPTER III

VIDEO

1. *Basic Concepts*.. 43
2. *Analog Video*... 45
3. *Digital Video*... 46
4. *Hardware and Software*..................................... 47
5. *Animation*... 51

CHAPTER 3

VIDEO

Motion video and computer based animation have become basic media for multimedia systems. In this chapter, we present concepts and development in these areas to develop understanding of the motion video and animation media. We describe analog and digital video and graphics animation with respect to the properties of human perception.

Basic Concepts

The human eye views pictures and motion pictures. The natural properties of the eye determines some essential conditions related to video systems. The televised image should convey spatial and temporal content of the scene so that the viewer has a sense of presence in the scene and participation in the events depicted.

Important features are as follows:

- **Vertical Detail and Viewing Distance.** It is the ratio of the picture width W to height H and is popularly known as aspect ratio. The conventional aspect ratio is 1.33 (4:3). The viewing distance D determines the angle h subtended by the picture height. This angle is usually measured by the ratio of the viewing distance to the picture height (D/H).

- **Horizontal Detail and Picture Width.** The picture width chosen for conventional television service is 4/3 x picture height. Using the aspect ratio, the horizontal field view can be calculated from the horizontal angle. The fields of view vary from system to system.

- **Total Detail Content of the Image.** The vertical resolution is equal to the number of picture elements separately presented in the picture height while the number of elements in the picture width is equal to the horizontal resolution times the aspect ratio. The product of the number of elements vertically and horizontally equals the total number of picture elements in the image.

- **Perception of Depth.** Perception of depth by eye depends upon the angular separation of the images received by the two eyes of the viewer. In the flat image of television, a considerable degree of depth perception is inferred from the perspective appearance of the subject matter. Further, the choice of the focal length of lenses and changes in depth of focus in a camera influence the depth of perception.

- **Luminance and Chrominance.** Colour vision is achieved through three signals, proportional to the relative intensities of red, green and blue light (RGB) in each portion of the scene. The colour encoding during transmission uses luminance and two chrominance signals.

- **Temporal Aspects of Illumination.** Another property of human vision is the boundary of motion resolution. In motion pictures, motion is the presentation of a rapid succession of the slightly different still pictures/frames. Between frames, the light is cut off briefly. To represent the visual reality, two conditions must be met. First, the rate of repetition of the images must be high enough to guarantee smooth motion from frame to frame. Second, the rate must be high enough so that the persistence of vision extends over the interval between flashes.

- **Continuity of Motion.** There are several standards for motion video signals which determine the frame rate to achieve proper continuity of motion. These are discussed in the later part of the chapter.

- **Flicker.** Through a slow motion, a periodic fluctuation of brightness perception, a flicker effect arises. To achieve continuous flicker free motion, a relatively high frequency is required. Movies, as well as television, apply some technical measures to work with lower motion frequencies.

- **Temporal Aspect of Video Bandwidth.** An important factor to determine which video bandwidth to use to transmit motion video is its temporal specification. Temporal specification depends on the rate of the visual system to scan pixels as well as on the human eye's scanning capabilities. For example, in a regular TV device, the time consumed in scanning lines and frames is measured in microseconds. In an HDTV (High Definition TV) device, however, a pixel can be scanned in less than a tenth of a millionth of a second. From the human visual perspective, the eye requires that a video frame be scanned every 1/25 second. This time is equivalent to the time during which a human eye does not see the flicker effect.

Analog Video

Analog video can come from a video disc player, video tape recorder or live television. There are two main standards for storing analog video. Phase Alternating Line (PAL) is used in UK, India and most of Europe. National Television System Committee (NTSC) is used in North and South America and Japan. There is also a third standard, SECAM used in France. Some video players and video disc players can now play both PAL and NTSC format videos.

In NTSC, a single frame consists of 525 horizontal scan lines. The picture is laid down on the screen in two frames, first odd numbered lines, then even at 60 frame/s or 60Hz. Using two frames like this is known as interlacing and it helps prevent flicker. Normally a computer monitor will be non-interlaced. That is, all the lines are drawn in one frame. PAL uses 625 lines with a frame rate of 25 frame/s. Like NTSC it is interlaced at 50Hz.

HDTV will probably be the next standard. This provides 1,200 lines, using a 16:9 aspect ratio (wide screen), rather than the 4:3 currently used. Currently there are three different HDTV standards, two of which are analog and the third digital.

Digital Video

As with images, there are a variety of digital video formats, mostly produced by commercial companies. Since digital video files are very large, the formats all include some kind of compression and formats such as AVI (Microsoft's Video for Windows) and Apple's QuickTime use several different kinds of compression.

The ISO compression standard for video is called MPEG (Moving Pictures Expert Group). An interim standard, MPEG-1, was released some time ago. MPEG-2 allows compression of the soundtrack with the video. There are three types of frames in MPEG, I (intra), P (predicted) and B (bi-directional) frames. The I frames are encoded as a still image, using DCT encoding. The P frames are predicted from the most recent I or P. The B frames are predicted from the closest two I or P frames (past and future). This helps to improve the signal to noise ratio (SNR), particularly at low bit rates, though it does increase computational complexity and bandwidth. A typical sequence of frame might be IBBPBBPBBPBBIBB.... since in order to decode a B frame you need the I or P frame that comes after it, the frames are not sent in sequential order. MPEG-1 audio will support 2 channels and sampling rates of 32,44.1 and 48kHz and the compression ratio is usually 1:6, giving 96 kbit/s. MPEG-2 is similar to MPEG-1, but has been extended to cover a wider range of applications. Whereas MPEG-1 was optimized for delivery on CD-ROM at 1.15 Mbit/s, MPEG-2 typically works at 4 Mbit/s. MPEG-2 audio will supply up to 5 full bandwidth channels and up to 7 commentary channels and also allows half sampling rates (e.g., 22.05kHz). MJPEG or Motion JPEG simply means each frame of the video has been compressed using JPEG.

DVI is a proprietary standard based on the Intel i750 chipset. It was used by a number of video capture cards, such as those by Action Media, but is now no longer supported.

Another ISO standard for video compression is H.261. This is designed to be used for video conferencing applications. This does not change very much from frame to frame and so predicting from one frame to the next can yield very high compression ratios.

AVI (Audio Video Interleaved) plays full motion video and audio in a small window at about 15 frames/sec (software alone). Like QuickTime, it also uses a number of different codecs. Video usually consists of a video track and two audio tracks. QuickTime is multi-track and so has the potential for a variety of uses. QuickTime uses a number of different compression schemes including a JPEG and a Kodak Photo-CD codec.

Hardware and Software

Analog

Video Cameras

Standard camcorders can be used to produce video provided they have a 'video out' facility. It is better to capture the video directly, rather than going through tape first. The signal from a video camera contains three channels of colour information and if these are transmitted separately, it is called RGB (red, green and blue). This gives the highest quality video. The video can also be transmitted as two chroma channels and one brightness. This is component video. When the signals are mixed, it is called composite video. S-VHS and Hi-8 video formats keep the colour and luminance information on two separate tracks, giving better quality than VHS.

Hi-8 is better quality than S-VHS and you can make unlimited VHS copies from it without the degradation that occurs when copying from VHS to VHS.

One of the most important accessories for a camcorder will be a zoom lens. This should be of as good quality as possible, as there are differences in resolution and optical quality. Standard consumer zoom lenses are usually around 6 or 8:1.

Video Discs/Laser Discs

Laser Discs have been on the market since 1978 and the largest market is in the US and Japan. They store movies, stills, or combinations of the two as analogue, either in NTSC or PAL format and offer much better quality than standard VHS tapes. They can also contain an analogue or digital sound track (with NTSC you can have both). Many of the current laser disc players can play either PAL or NTSC discs. The most common form of disc is 12" double sided, but there are also 8" and 5" discs available. The discs can have Constant Iinear Velocities (CLV) or Constant Angular Velocities (CAV). CLV is the most common form for movies as CLV discs can hold 60 minutes of video per side but they are only suitable for continuous play. CAV can hold only about half as much, as the recording density is reduced towards the outer edge, but individual frames can be randomly accessed and, therefore, these are often used for storing still images. A CAV disc can hold about 54,000 images. Unless it is stated, commercial discs are not resource discs and the images off them should not be used without permission from the copyright holders.

Video Overlay Boards

In order to display analogue video on a computer monitor, a video overlay board is required. Most boards have chroma keys where one colour is chosen and that colour becomes transparent allowing the video window to be seen through the computer image.

Video boards can often digitise frames from the video. For example, the Screen Machine II board (available for both PC and Mac) can capture a frame at full (736x560), half or quarter screen size to several file formats. When capturing a frame in this way, if you do not know what size the final image will be, capture it at full screen to maximise quality. If you know, however, that the final image will only be displayed at 320x200, for example, then capturing it at half size will give equally good quality.

There are two video capture boards, the Screen Machine II and Videologic's Capitulator. Although the screen machine card was over twice as expensive, it did not produce particularly better quality-captured images, but it did have more adjustment features.

The main advantage of using analogue video and an overlay board is that high quality full screen, full motion video will be available. However, delivering video in this way will be more expensive than digital video.

Digital

Hardware

DVI (Digital Video Interactive). It allows full screen playback of motion video at 30 frames/second and a synchronised sound track through a special card. Intel, who also produced the Action Media II DVI card which contains the i750 chipset, developed DVI. This card is no longer supported but software is available from Intel's FTP site to convert from DVI to AVI. Some of the compression techniques used in DVI have been incorporated into Intel's software based Indeo codec for video for Windows. Although this is software, its performance can be improved using hardware based on the i750, such as the Action Media card.

MPEG compression. There are a number of MPEG hardware compression and playback cards available for a range of systems. Hardware compression is much faster and allows for greater resolution than in software and is of better quality. Hardware playback also allows playback at more frames/second with larger windows and often supports the full MPEG audio capabilities, for example, the Reel Magic PC card provides video and sound playback in a 320x200 pixel window at 30 frames/second.

Other Accelerators: Hardware accelerators are available for Microsoft's Video for Windows, which will allow AVI files to be played full screen at 30 frames/second.

Software

QuickTime is an open proprietary standard designed by Apple. It uses a number of different codecs, including motion JPEG (MJPEG), RLE and Cinepak and runs in software alone on Macs, but players are also available for Microsoft Windows and Unix machines. The runtime players are freely distributable and available from Apple. Some authoring packages on the PC also support QuickTime movies. The shareware package Xanim plays QuickTime files (and many other formats) on Unix machines.

Video for Windows provides a format called Audio Video Interleaved (AVI), for which a number of codecs have been developed by Microsoft and third party developers. The video for windows software itself comes with tools to capture, edit and playback video sequences, though Microsoft in no longer developing these tools but will be relying on products from third party developers. Video for Windows was originally released with two codes, Video 1 and RLE (run length encoding), but other codecs are being released including Indeo from Intel and Cinepak. Both Indeo and Cinepak offer Mac compatibility and audio compression. Which codec you choose depends on the type of video you are compressing, the machine it will be delivered on and the delivery method, e.g., CD-ROM. Indeo, for example, offers better quality on high end machines than Video 1, but Video 1 may be better on low end machines. The runtime player for Video for Windows is freely distributable and can be obtained from Microsoft's FTP site and other Internet sites.

There are a number of MPEG encoders and decoders available in software alone, both 'professional' software and shareware or public domain. These mostly support MPEG-1 only and only video or audio, not both. Some of the packages will also convert between MPEG and other formats such as AVI and QuickTime. The Xing encoders/decoders only support I frame, rather than all three types of frames (IBP) and so some MPEG movies will not playback correctly on this software. Many of the packages are restricted to small windows for playback. For example, the VMPEG software (for DOS) can playback 16 frames/second in a 160x120 window on a 386 DX33. Players are available for most platforms including PC, Mac, X Windows, Amiga and Next machines.

Animation

To animate something is, literally, to bring it to life. A computer based animation is an animation performed by a computer using graphical tools to provide visual effects. We concentrate in this section on computer based animation because this kind of animation will become a part of multimedia systems. Simple animations can be done in many authoring packages by just putting an object on the screen and dragging it around with the mouse. The path is remembered and, on playback, the object moves along it. For many purposes, these very simple animations may be sufficient. For animation that is more complex, a specialised package may be necessary.

Basic Concepts

- **Input Process.** The drawing must be digitised through optical scanning so that the original drawing can be produced with a drawing programme in the first place. The drawing may need to be post-processed to avoid glitch arising from the input process.

- **Composition Stage.** This uses image composition techniques to combine the foreground and background figures together to generate the individual frames for the final animation

- **In-between Process.** The animation of movement needs a composition of frames with intermediate positions (intermediate frames) in between the key frames (the first and last frames). Computer animation programmes employ the same techniques through the interpolation.

There are many different languages for describing animation and new ones are constantly being developed. They fall into three categories:

- Linear-list notations
- General purpose languages
- Graphical languages

The description of these languages is beyond the scope of this book. Interested readers may refer books given in references for further reading.

Methods of Controlling Animation

Controlling animation is independent of the language used for describing it. Animation control mechanisms can employ different techniques:

- **Full Explicit Control.** The description of everything that occurs in the animation is provided either by specifying the simple changes, such as scaling, translation and rotation or by furnishing key frame information and interpolation methods to use between key frames.
- **Procedural Control.** It depends on the communication between various objects to determine their properties. Procedure control is a significant part of several other control mechanisms. In particular, in physically based systems, the position of one object may influence the motion of another. In actor based systems the individual actors may pass their positions to other actors to affect the other actor's behaviours.
- **Constrain Based Systems.** Motion of some objects are dependent upon the behaviour of other objects with which these are in contact. This compound motion may not be linear at all. Such motion can be modelled by constraints.
- **Tracking Live Action.** Trajectories of objects in the course of animation can also be generated by tracking live action.

- **Kinematics and Dynamics.** Kinematics refers to the position and velocity of points and dynamics takes into account the physical laws that govern kinematics.

Animations can be stored in standard digital movie formats such as AVI and QuickTime, but there are also formats which were designed especially with computer animation in mind, such as the FLI and FLC formats from Animator Pro. These are more advanced topics.

Review Questions

1. What is aspect ratio?
2. What is vertical resolution?
3. How can analog and digital video be differentiated?
4. How can flicker be avoided in a motion picture?
5. What are the basic hardware and software required for video?
6. What is animation? Explain with examples.

CHAPTER IV

Images and Graphics

1. *Introduction* 57
2. *Basic Concepts* 58
3. *Image Format* 59
4. *Graphics Format* 60
5. *File Format* 61
6. *Image Quality* 63
7. *Graphics System* 64
8. *Colour* 66

CHAPTER 4

Images and Graphics

Introduction

Images are needed in a wide variety of applications and computer supports it as per the needs of its users. An image is a spatial representation of an object, a two-dimensional or three-dimensional scene or another image. It can be real or virtual. A recorded image may be in a photographic analog video signal or digital format. In computer vision, an image is usually a recorded image such as video image, digital image or a picture. In computer graphics, an image is always a digital image. In multimedia applications, all formats can be presented. An image represents a still picture in digital form by using bits to specify the colour of each of the many pixels. An image has a given number of pixels across each row from left to right and a given number of rows of pixels from top to bottom. A given pixel's bits often specify its colour as amount of red, green and blue. In the case of monochrome image, one bit may specify that a pixel's colour is either black or white, whereas several bits may specify that pixel is one of a range of groups.

The distribution of digital images over communications networks will make our cultural heritage available to a wider audience than ever before. Creative use of digital imaging technology has the potential to change the nature of teaching and research. A common understanding of the principles and issues that pertain to the creation and distribution of digital image archives is required for this new field of activity to move ahead as a whole. In an area where the terminology and procedures are unfamiliar and where technology evolves rapidly, a basic outline of the issues and practices involved in creating a digital image is essential.

Basic Concepts

This section illustrates the technology and vocabulary of digital imaging as they relate to the development of image.

- **Digital Image.** A digital image is composed of a set of pixels (picture elements), similar to dots on a newspaper photograph or grains on a photographic print, arranged according to a predefined ratio of columns and rows. Each pixel represents a portion of the image in a particular colour, or shade of grey.

- **Pixels.** The points at which an image is sampled are known as picture elements, commonly abbreviated as pixels. The pixel values of intensity images are called gray scale levels (we encode here the "colour" of the image). The intensity at each pixel is represented by an integer and is determined from the continuous image by averaging over a small neighbourhood around the pixel location

- **Binary Valued Images.** The numbers 0 and 1 represent binary valued images, for example, black and white. When 8-bit are used to store each pixel value, the grey levels range from 0 (black) to 255 (white).

- **8-bit Image.** A digital image that can include as many as 256 possible colours. In this kind of image, 8 bits are allocated for the storage of each pixel, allowing 2 to the power of 8 (or 256) colours to be represented.

- **24-bit Image.** A digital image that can include approximately 16 million possible colours. In this kind of image, 24 bits are allocated for the storage of each pixel, allowing 2 to the power of 24 (or more than 16 million) colours to be represented.

- **Resolution.** The accuracy with which the original image is represented depends upon the number of pixels (in both height and width) making up an image. The higher the resolution of an image, the greater its clarity and definition. The number of dots per inch (dpi) used to display an image on a display device (monitor) or in print is called resolution at output. In brief, the number of pixels in a given area define the resolution of a digital image.

- **Dynamic Range.** Dynamic range (bit-depth) determines the number of colours or shades of grey (grey scale) that can be represented in a digital image. The specific colours used form the image's palette. The smallest unit of data stored in a computer is called a bit; dynamic range is a measurement of the number of bits used to represent each pixel in an image (and hence the maximum number of colours or shades of grey in its palette).

Image Format

There are different kinds of image formats. We shall consider the image format that comes out of an image frame grabber, i.e., the captured image format and the format when images are stored, i.e., the stored image format.

Captured Image Format

Images are converted to digital form using a scanner. During image capture, an image is read or scanned at a predefined resolution and dynamic range (digitising). The resulting file is then formatted and tagged so that it can be easily stored and retrieved. The image capture process is very labour-intensive and therefore costly. Image capture, combined with cataloguing and indexing, may account for 90 per cent of the cost of building an image database.

In image scan, it is important to attempt to maximise spatial resolution, colour quality and contrast ratio regardless of medium or system. Distinctions arise between media in the ways of achieving optimal quality in these areas but as ideals to be aimed at they are standard to all media. The values obtained for these three criterias are the combined products of the effects imposed by the choice of equipment for capture and manipulation and the expertise of the operator(s) involved.

Stored Image Format

Once an image is scanned, it is converted to a particular file format for storage. There are a number of widely used image formats, such as TIFF (Tagged Image/Interchange File Format), GIF (Graphic Image File format), PICT (Macintosh Picture, a storage format for digital images designed primarily for the Macintosh), TGA (True Vision Targa file), Sun raster (A file storage format used widely on Sun-3 computers), CGM (Computer Graphics Metafile) and the PhotoCD Imagepac. Image files include a certain amount of technical information, such as pixel dimensions and bit-depth. Images are stored in a two-dimensional array of values, in which each value represents the data associated with a pixel in the image. For a bitmap, this value is a binary digit. For a colour image, the value may be a collection of the red, green and blue components of the colour at the pixel in different intensity combinations.

If there is enough storage space, it is convenient to store an image in the form of RGB triples. Otherwise, it may be worth trying to compress the image in some way because high-resolution digital image files are very large (a 24-bit full-screen image to be displayed on a workstation can occupy 6 megabytes). Therefore, users often need to reduce the size of image files (see Compression).

Graphics Format

Graphic image formats are specified through graphic primitives and their attributes. In order to carry out graphics tasks, systems come equipped with their own particular sets of drawing instructions, or primitives as they are sometimes called. Some systems have comprehensive sets consisting of dozens of primitives to draw such things as lines, rectangles, circles, ellipses, polygons, arcs and other figures including text strings with two dimensional or three dimensional objects in a graphical image. These primitives are also capable of providing attributes to change line styles, to fill in areas with solid colours or hatching, to erase or display portions of a drawing, to rotate, move or reflect figures and so on with the help of single commands. Other systems have much more limited sets of primitives, perhaps allowing the display of only single lines in one style and colour. Systems differ not only on the output tasks they facilitate but also on the input tasks. Some will have no special primitives, others will cater for input from all sorts of sources.

In brief, a graphic package determines which primitives are supported. Packages such as SRGP (Simple Raster Graphics Package) generates bitmap/pixmap after taking graphics primitive and attributes but does not convert the graphical image into primitives and attributes after generating a bitmap/pixmap. In this case, bitmap/pixmap, after conversion into graphical image, is presented as a digital image format. On the other hand, PHICS (Programmer's Hierarchical Interactive Graphics System) and GKS (Graphical Kernel System) take graphical images specified through primitives and attributes, generate a graphical image in the form of pixmap and after image presentation, continue to work based on the object primitive/attribute representation.

File Format

Extension

In computer operating systems, a file name extension is an optional addition to the file name in a suffix of the form "xxx" where "xxx" represents a limited number of alphanumeric characters depending on the operating system. (In Windows 3.1, for example, a file name extension or suffix can have no more than three characters, but in Windows 95, it can have more). The file name extension allows a file's format to be described as part of its name so that users can quickly understand the type of file it is without having to open or try to use it. The file name extension also helps an application programme recognise whether a file is a type that it can work with.

Suffix

A suffix is something added at the end of a word that conditions its usage or meaning. In computer system file names, a suffix is a convention for having one or more characters appended to a file name (usually separated from the file name with a dot) so that it can be distinguished from other files or grouped together with similar types of files. For example, all files created with a WordPerfect word processor can be associated with a ".wpd" suffix. That way, a user can easily distinguish it as a file created with that word processor from files created with other tools and selectively process a number of similar files.

Different operating systems have different rules about how long the suffix part of a file name can be. DOS, Windows prior to Windows 95 and OS/2 prior to OS/2 Warp, limit suffix names to a maximum of three characters. UNIX systems, Windows 95 and Mac systems permit longer suffix names.

File

In data processing, using an office metaphor, a file is a related collection of records. For example, you might put the records you have on each of your customers in a file. In turn, each record would consist of fields for individual data items, such as customer name, customer number, customer address and so forth. By providing the same information in the same fields in each record (so that all records are consistent), your file will be easily accessible for analysis and manipulation by a computer programme. This use of the term has become somewhat less important with the advent of the database and its emphasis on the table as a way of collecting records and field data. In mainframe systems, the term data set is generally synonymous with file but implies a specific form of organisation recognised by a particular access method. Depending on the operating system, files (and data sets) are contained within catalogues, directories, or folders.

In any computer system, but especially in personal computers, a file is an entity of data available to system users (including the system itself and its application programmes) that is capable of being manipulated as an entity (for example, moved from one file directory to another). The file must have a unique name within its own directory. Some operating systems and applications describe files with given formats by giving them a particular file name suffix. For example, a programme or executable file is sometimes given or required to have an ". exe" suffix. In general, the suffixes tend to be as descriptive of the formats as they can be within the limits of the number of characters allowed for suffixes by the operating system.

Image Quality

Image quality is the cumulative result of the following:

- Scanning resolution
- Dynamic range of the scanned image
- The source material scanned
- The scanning device or technique used
- The skill of the scanning operator
- The final display device.

Image quality is often expressed in terms of resolution but other factors also affect the quality of an image file. Images are often stored at much higher quality than they are displayed on a monitor because most printing devices are capable of a much higher resolution than screen displays. When choosing quality levels, system designers must consider effective display and print resolutions and balance them with other image uses. The quality of a digital image can never exceed that of the source material from which the image is scanned. Differing film types contain different amounts of information.

When image capture takes place from a reproduction, the quality of the resulting digital image is limited by both that reproduction and the capability of the scanning device. Direct capture from original work offers image quality generally limited only by the capabilities of the scanning device or digital camera. It is certainly possible to get a higher quality image by scanning directly from the original work, but this is a time consuming process.

A key trade-off in defining an appropriate level of image quality is the balancing of file size and resulting storage requirements with quality needs. The higher the quality of an image, the more storage space it will occupy and the more system resources it will require. That is, higher bandwidth networks will be necessary to move it around, more memory will be needed in each work station to display it and the scanning process will be longer and costlier. Image compression provides a key to maintaining quality while using less storage space and systems resources (see Compression).

Graphics System

Like a general purpose computer system, a graphics system has three fundamental parts:

- **Hardware.** the equipment itself.
- **Software.** the instructions used to govern the workings of the hardware.
- **Documentation.** the descriptive information on the hardware and software given to enable to exploit the capabilities of the system to the full and also the documentation of image databases.

These three fundamental parts are interrelated and arranged in such a way which allows the production of images.

Hardware

A graphic system employs the following hardwares:

- **A processing unit.** This carries out the computation, i.e., computer/microprocessor.

- **Storage.** This stores programmes and data for future retrieval and is known as the secondary or external storage.

- **Graphical input devices.** These are required to present graphical information to the computer, for example, keyboard, light pens, mouse, joysticks, touchpanels, knobs, dials, sliders and scanners, etc.

- **Graphical output devices.** These are required to present information to the outer world, for example, Visual Display Unit (VDU). These devices can be divided into two categories:

  - Graphic displays for the real time interactive task. These include cathode ray tube (CRT), Direct View Storage Tube (DVST) displays, vector refresh displays, raster video displays and plasma panel displays, etc.

  - Graphic hardcopy devices for the drawing task. These devices include screen copiers, electrographic plotters, graphic printers, vector plotters and microfilm recorders, etc.

Software

An operating system and a language system are two elements of software. The operating system is a special programme which controls the operation of the devices as a whole. It schedules the work and ensures that any input, output, computation and storage is carried out in a correct and orderly fashion.

The language system allows us to create programmes reasonably quickly and easily by permitting programme writing in a style somewhat closer to human language than the abstract code used by the computer itself.

Documentation

The descriptive information on the hardware and software given to enable to exploit the capabilities of the system to the full needs to be accompanied by textual documentation to identify and describe them and aid in their management. The depth and complexity of this documentation will probably vary from one package to another.

There is a also need to create documentation of the image databases. Developers and users of documentation for image databases must distinguish among information that refers, first, to the original work, secondly, to photographic representations of that work. Thirdly, information pertains to the technical characteristics of a digital image (that may have been captured from the original or a photographic representation, or derived from an existing digital image file).

Careful documentation of (created by sub-sampling) image files is essential to manage the proliferation of multiple files depicting the same work in different formats and at different resolutions and dynamic range. Documentation standards incorporate expertise, both in formating database records for storage or interchange and in using structured vocabularies to represent data values for description and retrieval.

Colour

Colour is a vital component in presenting information. Unfortunately there is no known way to precisely specify the colour appearance. It is also difficult to quantify what it means for two colours to look the same when translating colour representations from device to device. This is especially acute when matching colours from a light-emitting device such as a CRT to a light reflecting media like a colour hardcopy. This results in problems when trying to reproduce specific colours on different devices.

Human Perception of Colour

Light is a physical quantity, measured by the distribution of power across the spectrum of visible light wavelengths. However, colour depends on the interaction of light with the human visual system and is thus a psychophysical quantity. For instance, human perception of colours may be radically altered depending on the viewing environment. The same image will look very different in the unlit interior of a movie theatre than in bright sunlight outside.

The human eye contains elements called rods and cones. Rods do not support colour vision and are sensitive to low levels of light (night vision). Cones come in three varieties, each responding to different ranges of wavelengths. Three primary colours can be chosen to stimulate the three types of cones to reproduce the perception of a particular colour; this is known as tristimulus colour. This means that only a small subset of the visible colour spectrum is needed to convince the eye that it is seeing a particular colour. Colour specifications such as RGB (red, green and blue) take advantage of this to economically describe colours, instead of specifying a power distribution across the entire spectrum. Unfortunately, no set of three primaries exists that can be combined to produce every colour.

The cones output colour signals that are relative to a "neutral" and perception is based on comparisons to this neutral. Neutral is constantly being redefined based on light sources, object colours, the visual environment around the viewer, the current state of the visual system and other factors. This is another reason that it is so hard to objectively quantify colour.

Colour Coordinate Systems

Different coordinate systems are available to represent colour specifications. The systems serve different purposes such as providing intuitive representations for humans or efficient representations for use in hardware. Unfortunately, each system distorts true colour representation in some way.

Different types of devices use different colour specifications and hence are capable of representing different colour gamut (the set of all possible colours that a device can produce). Also, individual devices may be calibrated differently and are subject to media-specific limitations in the range of colours they can accurately reproduce.

There are several colour specification schemes prevalent in computer and video systems, including RGB, HSI, CIE and NTSC YIQ. Knowing their purposes and limitations can help you understand which is best suited for a given stage in the production of your animation.

- **CIE.** The Commission Internationals de l'Eclairage (CIE) 1931 standard is the accepted objective standard for mapping a measured spectral distribution to tristimulus values. The CIE specification occupies 3D XYZ space. A 2D map called the CIE chromaticity standard is used to show the hues of the CIE standard – luminance (brightness) is not taken into account. The CIE chromaticity map shows the plane $X + Y + Z = 1$, so in the two dimensional space $x = X / (X + Y + Z)$ and $y = Y / (X + Y + Z)$. The CIE chromaticity chart is often used to show the gamut of other colour specifications as a subset of CIE space.

- **RGB.** The red/green/blue (RGB) colour specification is the most familiar to computer users. Specified percentages of red, green and blue primaries are added together to create the desired colour. These three primaries allow the broadest colour gamut possible with a three-primary system. This is a good system for discussing colour representation in hardware, but is not very intuitive for human use in specifying colour. For example, what mixture of red, green and blue is necessary to produce orange?

  RGB is a component video signal (a video system that conveys three colour component signals independently. Examples include RGB, YCbCr and MAC). This specification is the same used by video display hardware such as monitors and colour TVs, but the signal that is used to drive such devices is usually a composite signal (a video system that uses frequency interleaving to encode luminance and colour information into a single composite signal. Examples include NTSC, PAL and SECAM). Whenever the colour signal is converted from component to composite or composite to component, information is lost.

- **HSI.** The hue/saturation/intensity (HSI) model is an intuitive model for specifying colours. Hue is what people refer to as colour (red, yellow, etc.) and is represented as degrees on a "colour wheel" with values from 0 (red) to 120 (green) to 240 (blue) to 360 (red again). Saturation is the purity of the colour. Low saturation (0-20%) results in grey, regardless of the hue; middle saturation (40-60%) produces pastels; and high saturation (80-100%) results in vivid colours. Intensity is the brightness of a colour and ranges from 0% (black) to 100% (white). Intensity is also referred to as luminance or lightness.

Colour editing tools often allow users to specify colours using both RGB and HSI representations. You may also see very similar specifications such as hue/saturation/value (HSV), luminance/hue/saturation (LHS or HSL) and others.

- **NTSC YIQ.** The NTSC video standard uses a colour specification consisting of luminance (Y) and two colour difference signals called interphase and quadrature (I and Q). Luminance measures total brightness or intensity and is defined by the CIE standard to be

  Y = 0.59 Green + 0.30 Red + 0.11 Blue

  This is also the accepted formula for converting colour into grey scale. The colour difference signals are computed by subtracting multiples of the green and blue RGB components from the (scaled) red component.

  Such subtractive systems (colour specification system in which primary colours are subtracted from a reference colour to achieve a desired colour) use much less bandwidth than additive systems (colour specification system in which primary colours are added together to create a desired colour) such as RGB with no loss of information. This scheme has the added advantage that the colour difference signals can be bandwidth restricted and added as sub carriers to a primary luminance signal, which allows backward compatibility with black and white television signals when colour TV came into widespread popularity.

- **PAL.** This video standard uses a subtractive colour system similar to YIQ. However, it has a smaller colour gamut.

Colour and Computer Data

There are several common ways to associate colour with computer data. The most straightforward is true colour (a colour relationship scheme in which any colour value can be directly displayed, sometimes referred to as 16-bit or 24-bit colour), which directly associates data with any one of over 16 million colours. The more common colour association scheme is pseudocolour (a colour relationship scheme in which a colour table (a.k.a. colourmap) contains available colour values and an index into this table is used to refer to a colour. If a desired colour is not found in the table, it may be matched to the closest available entry or an existing entry may be overwritten. Also known as an index colour, colourmapped, or 8-bit (or less) colour system), which associates data with an index into a colourmap. Although each entry in the colourmap can be any one of over 16 million colours, colourmaps typically contain no more than 256 entries, so the number of data values distinguishable by colour is relatively low.

True colour displays can handle pseudocolour data with no problems. Pseudocolour displays cannot display true colour data directly, but can make reasonable approximations. The underlying data can still be true colour even if the displayed image is not. This is important to remember since most video formats are true colour and hence can record data with far more colour information than may be displayable on certain computer monitors.

Review Questions

1. What is a digital image?
2. What is pixel?
3. Define :
   (i) Dynamic range
   (ii) Binary valued images
   (iii) Resolution

4. Explain image format, captured image format and stored image format.

5. How can image quality be decided?

6. Define graphical system with examples.

7. Define colour, human perception of colour, colour coordinate systems and colour and computer data.

CHAPTER V

Compression

1. *Introduction* 75
2. *Image Compression* 76
3. *Compression Requirements* 78
4. *Compression Schemes* 80
5. *Some Basic Compression Techniques* 82
6. *Standards* 85

CHAPTER 5

Compression

Introduction

The development of compression standards is very important for the future of multimedia. In order to reduce the amount of storage space required for a document, surplus information should be reduced. There are three main ways of compressing image data. Text in document images may be converted from raster to ASCII. Line art can be vectorised using mathematical formulae. Bitonal and continuous tone images can be digitised and compressed using a variety of techniques. Reduction of the order of 2:1 to 50:1 can be achieved depending upon the quality required. It is utmost in case of video. Without compression, each frame of colour video will require a storage space of 7.4 Mbit. This will mean that only about 22 seconds of Full Screen, Full Motion (FSFM) video could be stored on a 600 MB optical disk. To play it back would require a transfer rate of 221 Mbit/s, which far exceeds the available rate of about 1.5 MBPS.

Both the uncompressed graphics, audio and video, pose the most difficult challenges as these require considerable storage capacity. That is, neither audio nor video files can tolerate apparent interruptions in their flow. In addition, both audio and video produce voluminous data files when they are digitised. The communication and computer industries have been grappling for years now with ways to overcome the audio/video file size dilemma. Data transfer of uncompressed video data over digital networks requires very high bandwidth to be provided for a single point to point communication. To provide feasible and cost effective solutions, most multimedia systems handle compressed digital and audio data streams.

Many compression techniques are in use in today's products, while other methods are still under development or are only partly realised. Nowadays, the most important compression techniques are JPEG (for single pictures), H.261 (for video), MPEG (for video and audio) and proprietary developments including HQ Learn's DVI (for still images, audio and video), Intel's Indeo, Microsoft's Video for Windows, IBM's Ultimotion Matinee, Apple's QuickTime or DigiCipher II developed by General Instruments Corporation and AT&T.

Image Compression

There are three main ways of converting image data. Text in document images may be converted from raster to ASCII format. Line art can be vectorised, using mathematical formulae. Bitonal and continuous tone still images can be digitised and encoded using a variety of established algorithms. Reductions of the order of 2:1 to upto 50:1 are achievable using the existing international standards. The actual compression achieved for an individual image depends upon its content and the quality required when an image is restored.

Text Conversion

Raster to ASCII conversion is carried out using some form of character recognition technology. Optical Character Recognition (OCR) for fixed pitched fonts was based on matching the scanned characters to standards held in memory. A standard was required for each font hence as the number of fonts grew, the size of library increased and, therefore, the time required for selecting the correct font and matching the characters also increased.

In contrast omni font OCR is based on the use of techniques from artificial intelligence and is therefore also known as Intelligent Character Recognition (ICR). In this, each character is recognised by the presence and absence of sets of particular features that are independent of typeface and font size. ICR systems can handle proportional spacing, tables and graphics and in some cases hand written characters.

Vectorisation

Vector data treats an image as a series of points and mathematical functions that describe geometric figures such as lines, circles or arcs. The process of converting raster data into vector data is known as vectorisation. It is suitable for images containing alpha-numeric characters and line drawings such as forms, organisation charts, flow diagrams, circuit diagrams, maps and cartoons.

Image Compression

Images that are not suitable for conversion to text or vectorisation (complex line arts and continuous tone images) are compressed using standard algorithms to eliminate as much unnecessary information as possible. Individual still images are compressed by spatial redundancy techniques. These remove repetition of patterns within each frame (intraframe compression).

Compression in which the data can be recovered without a loss is known as lossless compression. Greater compression can be achieved by using more sophisticated methods in which sampling techniques are used to represent areas of the image. In some of these methods – known as lossy methods – the data is not exactly recoverable.

In practice, compression standards such as JPEG and MPEG and H.261 use a mixture of techniques. A typical sequence would be:

- Analogue to digital conversion
- Processing using an algorithm such as Discrete Cosine Transform (DCT) to transform the data into a different mathematical domain that is more easily compressed
- Quantisation to reduce the precision at which the output is stored (e.g., by reducing the number of bits per pixel)
- Entropy encoding (e.g., run-length) to remove any redundant information in the resulting data stream.

All these steps are reversed in the decompression process.

Compression can be:

Symmetric. If decompression is a step-by-step reversal of compression.

Asymmetric. This type of compression takes much longer than decompression and needs a much more powerful computer.

Compression Requirements

Images have considerable higher storage requirements than text; audio and video have even more demanding properties for data storage. Neither audio nor video files can tolerate apparent interruptions in their flow. To compare data storage and bandwidth requirements of different visual media (text, graphics and image), the following specifications are based on a typical window size of 640×480 pixels on a screen:

- For the representation of text, two bytes are used for each character. Each character is displayed using 8×8 pixels, which is sufficient for the display of ASCII characters.

- For the presentation of vector graphics, a typical still image is composed of 500 lines. Its horizontal position, vertical position and an 8-bit attribute field for third dimension define each line. The horizontal axis is represented using 10 bits [log2 (640)] and the vertical axis is coded using 9 bits [log2 (480)].

- In very simple colour display modes, a single pixel of a bitmap can be represented by 256 different colours, therefore, one byte per pixel is needed.

For continuous media the amount of storage required for one second of playback can be derived as follows:

- An uncompressed audio signal of telephone quality is sampled at 8kHz and quantised with 8-bits per sample. This leads to a bandwidth requirement of 64-kbits/second and storage requirement of 64 kbits to store one second of playback.

  An uncompressed stereo audio signal of CD quality is sampled at a rate of 44.1 kHz and is quantised with 16 bits per sample; hence, the storage requirement is 44.1kHz × 16 bits = 705.6 × 10E3 bits to store one second of playback and the bandwidth requirement is 705.5 × 10E3 bits/second.

- According to the European PAL (phase Alternating Line) standard, 625 lines and 25 frames per second define video. The luminance and colour difference signals are encoded separately. The resulting digital data streams are transformed using a multiplexing technique (4:2:2). CCIR recommendation 601 specifies digital video, a sampling rate of 13.5 MHz is used for luminance Y. The sampling rate for chrominance (R-Y and B-Y) is 6.75 MHz. If the result is a uniform 8-bit coding of each sample, the bandwidth requirement is (13.5 MHz +6.75 MHz +6.75 MHz) × 8bits = 216 Megabits/second. HDTV doubles the number of lines and uses an aspect ratio of 16/9. This leads to a data rate which increases by a factor of 5.33, compared to today's TV rate.

The storage requirements for the PAL standard, assuming the image resolution of 640 × 480 pixels and 3 bytes/pixel to encode the luminance and chrominance components is 640 pixels × 480 pixels

× 3 bytes = 921,600 bytes. To store 25 frames/second, the storage requirement is 23.04 megabytes.

Compression Schemes

Compression techniques fit into different categories. For their use in multimedia systems, we can distinguish among lossless, lossy and hybrid encoding. There has been a great deal of research and many implementations using software, hardware, or both for a variety of compression methods. Research continues with further improvements expected using fractal and wavelet and other time and space domain techniques.

Lossless

In these compression schemes, the original representation can be perfectly recovered. For text, lossless methods may achieve a 2:1 reduction. For bi-level images 15:1 compression ratio is achieved. These approaches are also called entropy coding decomposition techniques. For example, Huffman coding uses fewer bits for more common message symbols and run length encoding replaces strings of the same symbol with a count per symbol pair.

Lossy

This compression involves encoding into a form that takes up relatively small amount of space but which can be decoded to yield a representation that humans find similar to the original. An example is the sound source coding where sound is transformed from time dependent to frequency dependent sound concatenations.

Predictive

This approach, like Differential Pulse Code Modulation (DPCM), involves predicting subsequent values by observing previous ones and transmitting only the usually small differences between actual and predicted data. An example involves motion compensation. Successive frames in a video sequence are often quite similar or have blocks of pel shifted from one frame to the next, for example, as the camera pans or a person moves. Although it is computationally expensive to analyse images and yield motion vectors, parallel computers can help in the processing.

The following four steps describe one image compression:

1. Preparation includes analog-to-digital conversion and generating an appropriate digital representation of the information. An image is divided into blocks of 8 × 8 pixels and represented by a fixed number of bits per pixel.

2. Processing is actually the first step of the compression process which makes use of sophisticated algorithms. A transformation from the time to the frequency domain can be performed using DCT. In the case of motion video compression, interframe coding uses a motion vector for each 8 × 8 block.

3. Quantisation processes the results of the previous step. It specifies the granularity of the mapping of real numbers into integers. This process results in a reduction of precision. This can also be considered as the equivalence of the u-law and A-law, which apply to audio data [JN84]. In the transformed domain, the coefficients are distinguished according to their significance. For example, they could be quantised using a different number of bits per coefficient.

4. Entropy encoding is usually the last step. It compresses a sequential digital data stream without loss. For example, a sequence of zeroes in a data stream can be compressed by specifying the number of occurrences followed by the zero itself.

Processing and quantisation can be repeated iteratively several times in feedback loops, such as in the case of Adaptive Differential Pulse Code Modulation (ADPCM). After compression, the compressed video builds a data stream, where a specification of the image starting point and an identification of the compression technique may be part of this data stream; the error correction code may also be added to the stream. Decompression is the inverse process of compression.

Some Basic Compression Techniques

Hybrid compression techniques are a combination of well known algorithms and transformation techniques that can be applied to multimedia systems.

- In **Run length coding** a substantial reduction of data can be achieved. Sampled images, audio and video data streams often contain sequences of the same bytes. These repeated byte sequences can be replaced with the number of occurrences.

- **Sub band coding** can exploit the fact that humans have different sensitivities to various spatial and temporal frequency combinations. The idea is to separate the different frequency combinations using filters and then to code with greater fidelity the frequencies those humans pay particular attention to.

- **Transform coding** is another approach related to human handling of frequency. This usually involves spatial frequencies as in single images. The most powerful approach is Discrete Cosine Transform (DCT), which is related to the fast Fourier transform. Lower spatial frequencies must be carefully coded while higher frequencies need less detailed coding.

- **In importance oriented compression** the principle is to consider those parts of an image that humans are better tuned to as more important. An example of this approach is to filter images in order to getting rid of details that cannot be perceived. Another technique is to allocate more bits to encode important parts of an image, such as where edges occur, than to encode large homogenous regions.

- **Sub sampling** is also based on characteristics of human vision. It involves using lower sampling rate for chrominance and luminance. Interpolation in decoder results in a full but approximate reconstruction of the original.

- **Vector quantisation** also relates to patterns in an image representation. Clearly, higher level descriptions where symbols refer to large structures can take much less space than raster forms, this translates into the fact that vector quantisation can lead to higher compression. It takes two dimensional vector values, for example, 4×4 blocks and maps them into a code symbol. Thus, code books are developed for images, recording the most important vectors and all data vectors are mapped to the nearest code book entry, minimising m.s.e. Decoding involves fast lookup to replace coded entries with vectors from the code book. Encoding usually takes a good deal of computation, so near optimal code books can be developed.

- In **hybrid coding** various compression techniques can be combined, for example, in DCT and DPCM sub band coding and vector quantisation, a 10:1 compression ratio can be achieved. Systems for video compression often apply motion compensation for temporal compression, transform coding for spatial compression and Huffman, run length coding for statistical compression.

- **Fractal block coding.** Hybrid coding suffers two types of distortions namely blocking artifacts and mosquito noise, both of which become annoying as bit rate decreases. In order to avoid these artifacts, fractals (images that can be described by a set of rules specified with a relatively small number of bits) allow compression of natural scenes where the underlying structure matches this type of model. Very high compression ratios of the order of 1000:1 can be achieved. However, extensive computation is required for encoding while decoded images may be acceptable to human judgement, there is usually some quality loss.

The coding procedure consists of image partition and fractal block coding. The partition is simultaneously performed into non-overlapping range block of size B×B and into overlapping domain blocks with a typical size 2B×2B. The blocks are further classified into shade, midrange and edge and then fractal coding procedure is applied, which results in a fractal code. The fractal code is actually an affine transformation, which is a collection of translation, rotation and scaling and describes the relation between particular parts of the fractal (i.e., the original digital image). Decoding of a fractal coded image is simpler than the encoding and consists of iterating the fractal code on an initial image until a stable decoded image is obtained. Depending upon the nature of the original image, a compressed bit rate of 0.2-0.72 bits per pel can be achieved.

- **Wavelet transform coding** is a new compression technology and offers a compression ratio of nearly 200:1. Wavelets remove blocking artifacts as their basic functions overlap one another and decay smoothly to zero at their ends. In wavelet transformation, the input signal is split into a number of bands with the help of low-pass filters and high-pass filters. The low-pass filter L and the high-pass filter H are applied to the image in both the horizontal and vertical directions. The filter outputs are sub sampled by a factor of two, generating three orientation selective high pass sub bands, HH, HL, LH and a low pass sub band LL. The process is then repeated on the LL band to generate the next level of the decomposition, etc. Four octaves of decomposition lead to 13 sub bands. In general, the wavelet transform requires much less hardware to implement in comparison to DCT implementation. To compress the image data, one must decide which coefficients to send and how many bits to use to code them? Each group of transform coefficients is gathered according to their spatial position and quantisation is executed with a uniform quantiser. Then scanning of the quantised transform is carried out from lower frequency blocks to higher frequency blocks followed by variable length coding. This scanning path is determined to increase zero run by which the efficiency of entropy coding is improved. This approach is analogous to the conventional transform coding approach using DCT. The scheme achieves better compression ratios for a given picture quality and is simpler to implement in hardware to achieve real time performance for video sequences. The errors introduced in this scheme are less visually annoying than for DCT compressed images due to the lack of blocking effects.

Standards

In the following sections, the most relevant work in standardisation bodies concerning image and video coding is outlined. In the framework of ISO/IECJTC1/SC2/WG8, four subgroups were established in May 1988: JPEG (Joint Photographic Experts Group working on coding algorithms for still images); JBIG (Joint Bi Level Expert Group working on the progressive processing of bi level coding algorithms); CGEG (Computer Graphics Expert Group working on coding principles); and MPEG (Motion Pictures Experts Group working on the coded representation of motion video). Standardisation of video compression techniques has become a high priority because only a standard can reduce the high cost of video compression codes and resolve the critical problem of interoperability of equipment from different manufacturers. The existence of a standard is often the trigger to the volume production of VLSI ICs necessary for significant cost reductions. There are three types of standards namely JPEG, MPEG and H.261.

JPEG (Joint Photographic Experts Group)

Continuous tone still images are compressed using JPEG, a collaboration between ITU-T and ISO to develop a general purpose compression standard for both grey scale and colour images. The objective of JPEG was focused exclusively on still image compression. The distinction between still and moving image is thin. A video sequence can be thought of as a sequence of still images to be coded individually but displayed sequentially at video rate. However, the sequence of still images approach has the disadvantage that it fails to take into consideration the extensive frame-to-frame redundancy present in all video sequences. The activity of JPEG played a considerable role in the beginning of MPEG since both groups were originally in the same working group of ISO and there has been considerable overlap in membership.

JPEG usually involves sequential encoding using forward DCT, scalar quantisation and Huffman coding. The decoder simply reverses the process.

JPEG is designed for compressing either full-colour or gray-scale images of natural, real-world scenes. It works well on photographs, naturalistic artwork and similar material. It is not very effective on lettering, simple cartoons or line drawings. JPEG handles only still images. There is a related standard called MPEG for motion pictures.

JPEG is "lossy," meaning that the decompressed image is not quite the same as the one you started with. JPEG is designed to exploit known limitations of the human eye, notably the fact that small colour changes are perceived less accurately than small changes in brightness. Thus, JPEG is intended for compressing images that will be looked at by humans. If machines analyse these images, the small errors introduced by JPEG may create problem, even if they are invisible to the eye.

A useful property of JPEG is that the image-maker can reduce or increase the file size against output image quality. Extremely small files can also be created at the cost of quality. This is useful for applications such as indexing image archives.

Another important aspect of JPEG is that decoders can trade off decoding speed against image quality by using fast but inaccurate approximations to the required calculations. Some viewers obtain remarkable speedups in this way. (Encoders can also trade accuracy for speed, but there is usually less reason to make such a sacrifice when writing a file.)

Why JPEG?

It makes your image files smaller and to store 24-bit-per-pixel colours data instead of 8-bit-per-pixel data. It is especially useful for transmitting files across networks and for archiving libraries of images. Being able to compress a 2 Mbytes full-colour file down to, say, 100 Kbytes makes a big difference in disk space and transmission time. In addition, JPEG can easily provide 20:1 compression of full-colour data.

Disadvantage of JPEG is that it takes longer to decode and view a JPEG image than to view an image of a simpler format such as GIF. Thus using JPEG is essentially a time/space trade off: you give up some time in order to store or transmit an image more cheaply.

Nevertheless, it is worth noting that when network transmission is involved, the time saving from transferring a shorter file can be greater than the time needed to decompress the file.

The second fundamental advantage of JPEG is that it stores full colour information: 24 bits/pixel (16 million colours). GIF, the other image format widely used on the net, can only store 8 bits/pixel (256 or fewer colours). As full-colour hardware is getting cheaper all the time and JPEG photos look much better than GIF on such hardware, therefore, within a couple of years, GIF will probably seem as obsolete as black-and-white MacPaint format does today. Furthermore, JPEG is far more useful than GIF for exchanging images among people with widely varying display hardware because it avoids prejudging how many colours to use. Hence JPEG is considerably more appropriate than GIF for use as an internet and world wide web standard photo format.

MPEG (Motion Picture Experts Group)

MPEG is a group of people that meet under ISO to generate standards for digital video (sequences of images in time), audio compression and audiovisual synchronisation. Digital video compression is one of the key issues in video coding, enabling efficient interchange and distribution of visual information. New applications in the field of communication, multimedia and digital television broadcasting require highly efficient, robust and flexible digital video compression and encoding techniques. The integration of motion video as an integral part of multimedia environment is technologically one of the most demanding tasks due to the high data rates and real-time constraints.

In particular, they define a compressed bit stream, which implicitly defines a decompressor. However, the compression algorithms are upto individual manufacturers and the scope of a publicly available international standard. The three original work items of the group coding upto 1.5,10 and 40 Mb/s were nicknamed as MPEG-1, 2 and 3 respectively. The group dropped the MPEG-3 work item when it became apparent that functionalities supported by the MPEG-2 requirements made it redundant. The current MPEG-4 work item targets audiovisual coding at very low bit rates.

MPEG and JPEG sound the same and they are part of the same subcommittee of ISO alongwith JBIG (for binary image compression like faxes) and MHEG (for multimedia data standards like integrating stills, video, audio, text, etc.).

To use MPEG video files, you need a personal computer with sufficient processor speed, internal memory and hard disk space to handle and play the typically large MPEG file (which has a file name suffix of .mpg). You also need MPEG viewer or client software that plays MPEG files. (Note that .mp3 file suffixes indicate MP3 (MPEG-1 audio layer-3) files, not MPEG-3 standard files.) You can download shareware or commercial MPEG players from a number of sites on the web.

The MPEG standards are an evolving set of standards for video and audio compression developed by the Moving Picture Experts Group (MPEG).

MPEG-1

It was designed for coding progressive video at a transmission rate of about 1.5 million bits per second. It was designed specifically for Video CD and CD-I media. MPEG-1 audio layer-3 (MP3) has also evolved from early MPEG work.

MPEG-1 is a standard specifying the systems, video and audio. The system addresses the problem of combining one or more data streams from the video and audio parts of the MPEG-1 standard with timing information to form a single stream. This is an important function because, once combined into a single stream, the data are in a form well suited to digital storage or transmission.

Video specifies a coded representation that can be used for compressing video sequences to bit rates around 1.5 Mbit/s. This is developed to operate principally from storage media offering a continuous transfer rate of about 1.5 Mbit/s. Nevertheless it can be used more widely than this because the approach taken is generic.

Audio specifies a coded representation that can be used for compressing audio sequences (both mono and stereo). Input audio samples are fed into the encoder. The mapping creates a filtered and sub sampled representation of the input audio stream.

MPEG-1 and also 2 define techniques for compressing digital video by factors varying from 25:1 to 50:1. The compression is achieved using five different compression techniques:

- The use of a frequency based transform called Discrete Cosine Transform (DCT).
- Quantisation, a technique for losing selective information (sometimes known as lossy compression) that can be acceptably lost from visual information.
- Huffman coding, a technique of lossless compression that uses code tables based on statistics about the encoded data.
- Motion compensated predictive coding, in which the differences in what has changed between an image and its preceding image are calculated and only the differences are encoded.
- Bi-directional prediction, in which some images, are predicted from the pictures immediately preceding and following the image.

MPEG-2

MPEG-2 was designed for coding interlaced images at transmission rates above 4 million bits per second. MPEG-2 is used for digital TV broadcast and DVD. An MPEG-2 player can handle MPEG-1 data as well.

MPEG-3

A proposed MPEG-3 standard, intended for High Definition TV (HDTV), was merged with the MPEG-2 standard when it became apparent that the MPEG-2 standard met the HDTV requirements. An MPEG-4 standard is in the final stages of development and release. It is a much more ambitious standard and addresses speech and video synthesis, fractal geometry, computer visualisation and an Artificial Intelligence (AI) approach to reconstructing images. An MPEG-7 is being discussed.

H.261

H.261 is video-coding standard published by the ITU (International Telecom Union) in 1990. It was designed for data rates which are multiples of 64Kbit/s and is sometimes called p × 64Kbit/s (p is in the range 1-30). These data rates suit ISDN lines for which this video codec was designed. H.261 is currently the most widely used international video compression standard for video telephony on ISDN telephone lines. The standard describes the video coding and decoding methods for the moving picture component of an audiovisual service at the rates of p*64 kbps where p is in the range of 1 to 30. The standard is most suitable for applications using circuit switched networks as their transmission channels. This is understandable as ISDN with both basic and primary rate accesses was the communication channel considered within the framework of the standard. H.261 is usually used in conjunction with other control and framing standards such as H221, H230, H242 and H230.

Review Questions

1. What do you understand by image and its compression?
2. What are the different techniques in use for image compression?
3. Differentiate among JPEG, MPEG and H.261.
4. How are the compression requirements analysed?
5. Why is JPEG used?

CHAPTER VI

Storage Media

1. *Introduction* 93
2. *Magnetic Media* 94
3. *Principle* 94
3. *Magnetic-Optical Disk Method* 102
4. *Optical Disks and Their Basic Technology* 103
5. *Data Standards* 110

CHAPTER 6

Storage Media

Introduction

Magnetic media has been used for a long time. It has offered large storage capacities, low cost per bit and medium access times. Current magnetic data storage carriers take the form of floppy disks or hard disks and are used as secondary storage media. But audio and video, either in compressed form or uncompressed form, require higher storage capacity than the other media and the storage cost for such continuous media using traditional storage methods is significantly higher.

Optical storage media offer a higher storage density at a lower cost. As optical storage improves, it will make inroads into the area of mass storage devices like hard disks. One trend that is appearing is a move towards CD-ROM and optical storage medium. Many software companies offer both, operating systems software and application software on CD-ROM today.

The audio compact disk is a commercially successful product in the entertainment industry. The computer industry has benefited from this development, especially when audio and video have to be stored digitally in the computer. This technology has been the main catalyst for the whole development of multimedia in computing because it is used in the multimedia external devices. For example, external devices such as video recorders and DAT recorders (Digital AudioTape) can be used for the multimedia systems.

Magnetic Media

Disk Storage

Disks are used to store data, operating systems, application software and systems software. Whereas the primary form of storage in the early days of computing was magnetic tape, this has been replaced by the predominantly disk-based medium today. The reasons for this trend are:

- decreasing cost per bit
- reliability
- reduced access times
- higher transfer rates (more data per second)
- reduced size and power requirements
- increased capacity.

Principle

Disk storage systems are essentially based on magnetic properties. This is the same principle as used in cassette tape recorders. A rotating disk is coated with fine magnetic particles. When writing data, a write head magnetizes the particles on the disk surface as either north or south poles. When reading data, a read head converts the magnetic polarisation's on the disk surface to a sequence of pulses. The read and write heads are generally combined into a single head unit. There may be more than one read/write head. Consider the example shown below, where a group of heads is used to write data onto concentric rings on the magnetic drum. In this example, the heads are fixed (non-moveable).

Figure 6.1 Magnetic Drum

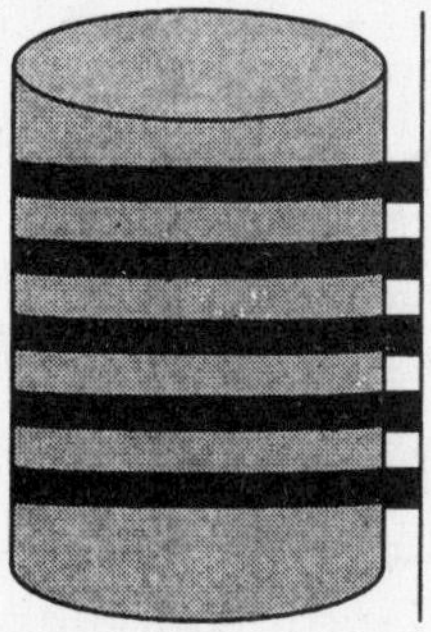

The problem with this drum approach is limited capacity. The increase in the capacity requires an increase in the circumference size of the drum or more read/write heads.

A more common approach used today is to use a read/write head attached to a moveable arm which steps across (by small increments) the surface of the disk. The disk is a platter coated with magnetic particles. Early drives were large. Later on, smaller rigid disk drivers were developed with one fixed and one removable pack. Each pack held about 30 megabytes (MB) of data and became known as the Winchester drive. Most Winchester drives have the following common features:

- the disk and read/write heads are enclosed in a sealed airtight unit
- the disk(s) spin at 3,600 revolutions per minute
- the read/write heads do not actually touch the disk surface
- the disk is lubricated (heads fly above when the disk is up to speed)

- the disk surface contains a magnetic coating
- the disk surface (platters) is fixed.

Data is arranged as a series of concentric rings. Each ring is called a track, is subdivided into a number of sectors, each sector holding a specific number of data elements called bytes or characters.

Figure 6.2 A Track Subdivided into Sectors

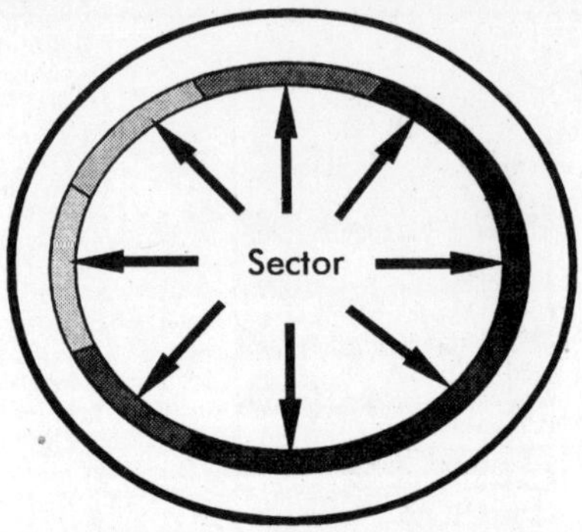

The smallest unit that can be written to or read from the disk is a sector. There is a delay involved on receiving a read or write request. This delay is because of the time taken by the required sector to reach the read/write head. This is known as rotational latency and on an average is one half of the period of revolution.

The storage capacity of the disk is determined as number of tracks, number of sectors, bytes per sector and number of read/write heads.

Disk Drive Characteristics

The characteristics of a disk drive may be illustrated as below:

- **Tracks and Sectors.** The disk is divided into concentric rings called tracks. A track is thus one complete rotation of the disk underneath the read/write head. The width of a track is determined by the size of the read/write head and the distance between tracks is determined by the mechanics of the stepper motor which controls the positioning of the arm to which the read/write head is attached. Each track is subdivided into a number of sectors. Each sector contains a specific number of bytes or characters. Typical sector capacities are 128, 256, 512,

1024 and 4096 bytes. Increasing the number of tracks is one way to increase the storage capacity of a disk drive. Often the physical size of the disk imposes space restrictions which make this impractical. The most common choice is increasing the number of sectors per track (from 17 to 34) or increasing the number of bytes stored in each sector.

- **Bad Blocks.** The drive maintains an internal table which holds the sectors or tracks which cannot be read or written to because of surface imperfections. This table is called the bad block table and is created when the disk surface is initially scanned during a low-level format.

- **Partitions.** A disk partition is a sub-division of the disk into one or more areas. Each partition can be used to hold a different operating system. The computer system boots from the active partition and software provided allows the user to select which partition is the active one.

- **Sector Interleave.** This refers to the numbering of the sectors located in a track. A one to one interleave has sectors numbered sequentially, 0, 1, 2, 3, 4, etc. The disk drive rotates at a fixed speed, 3,600rpm, which means that there is a fixed time interval between each sector. A slow computer can issue a command to read sector 0, storing it in an internal buffer. Whilst it is doing this, the drive makes available sector 1 but the computer is still busy storing sector 0. Thus the computer will now have to wait one full revolution till sector 1 becomes available again. Renumbering the sectors like 0, 8, 1, 9, 2, 10, 3, 11, etc., gives a 2:1 interleave. This means that sectors are alternated, giving the computer slightly more time to store sectors internally than previously.

- **Drive Controller.** A special peripheral card called a drive controller manages the drive. It may handle multiple drives or only a single drive. The controller is often responsible for issuing commands to position the read/write head (especially in MFM and RLL drives). In SCSI and IDE drives, the controller is simplified and the intelligence is placed onto the drive itself. These drives offer sophisticated features like caching and hot fix (write errors are redirected to another free sector).

- **Rotation Speed.** This refers to the speed of rotation of the disk. Most hard disks rotate at 3,600 rpm. To increase data transfer rates, higher rotational speeds, or multiple read/write heads arranged in parallel, or disk arrays (multiple disks arranged in parallel) are required.

- **Low/High level Formatting.** Low level formatting is placing track and sector information, plus bad block tables and other timing information on the disk. Sector interleave can also be specified at this time. High level formatting involves writing directory structures and file allocation tables to the disk. Often this also means transferring the boot file for the operating system onto the hard disk.

- **Access Time.** Access time refers to how soon the drive makes data available once issued with the command to read the data. Once a read command is issued, the drive must position the read/write head at the appropriate track number and wait for the correct sector to arrive.

- **Latency.** This refers to the delay between the read/write request and the appearance of the required sector under the read/write head.

- **Timing Tracks.** In larger drives used on main frame computers, the disk drives often had timing tracks written. These tracks were used for alignment purposes to ensure that the read/write head was accurately positioned over the track. The read/write head was moved until the pulses picked up from the timing head were at a maximum. This meant that the read/write head was correctly positioned over the data track. Newer and more accurate mechanisms have tended to make this obsolete.

Disk Drive Types

Following are various drive types available for IBM-PC compatible computers:

- **MFM (Modified Frequency Modulation).** These drive types were the first to be made for the IBM-XT model. Storage capacity was 30MB with access types of about 30ms. Capacity ranges were from about 10MB to 80MB. Due to their design, it was costly to make drives any larger. MFM refers to the encoding technique used to store data on the disk. They are all but replaced by IDE.

- **RLL (Run Length Encoding).** This is similar to MFM drives except that the encoding technique used to store data essentially doubles the capacity of an MFM drive. Few, if any, manufacturers still make MFM or RLL drives today.
- **ESDI (Enhanced Small Disk Interface).** These drive types range in capacity from about 80MB to about 300MB. They are becoming less common. The advantage they have over RLL or MFM drives is higher data transfer rates (about twice as fast).
- **SCSI (Small Computer Systems Interface).** The common drive choice for servers or high-end workstations, drive capacities range from 100MB to 4GB. They have fast access times and high data transfer rates, but are expensive. One advantage of these drives is that a single controller can handle seven drives.
- **IDE (Integrated Disk Electronics).** A common drive used today for workstations with capacities of 40MB to 1000MB. Good access times of about 20ms but slower data transfer rates than SCSI drives. Drives are reasonably cheap but the controllers can only handle a maximum of two drives (some will handle only one).

Floppy Drives

The floppy drive uses a thin circular ceramic disk for data storage. The disk is coated with magnetic particles and is flexible (hence the term floppy). The disk rotates at 360rpm. A read/write head makes physical contact with the disk surface. Data is recorded as a series of tracks subdivided into sectors.

Typical values for IBM-PC compatibles are given in the following table:

Table 6.1 Typical IBM-PC compatibles values

Size	Capacity	Tracks	Sectors
5.25	360KB	40	9
5.25	1.2MB	80	15
3.5	720KB	40	18
3.5	1.44MB	80	18

There are two main methods of identifying the beginning sector of a track as given below:

- **Hard Sectored Floppy.** In hard sectored, the start of each sector is identified by a physical hole. A light is shone through the hole and picked up on the other side by a detector. As the disk rotates, this causes a sequence of pulses to occur as the sector ID holes allow the light to pass through to the detector. The holes are called index holes. This method was used in the Apple II computer.

- **Soft Sectored Floppy.** In soft sectored, only one index hole is used and each sector is preceded with data bytes which identify the sector number. This format is used in IBM-PC compatible computers.

Hard Disks

Hard disk drives use a thicker non-flexible disk. The disk is made from aluminium or ceramic material and coated in magnetic particles. The disk rotates at a much higher speed (3,600rpm). In addition, multiple disks are stacked on top of each other (with a gap in between), with a read/write head allocated for each surface (top and bottom). Storage capacities range from 10MB (first PC disk used in XT) to several gigabytes.

- **Exchangeable Disks.** The disks are provided as removable cartridges that can be removed and inserted into the drive. The drive unit contains the motor drive, electronics and read/write heads. When the cartridge is inserted, the read/write heads are positioned to make contact with the disk platters inside the cartridge pack. This allows a flexible method of data storage. As each disk pack becomes full, it can be removed and a new pack inserted to handle the next lot of transactions, etc.

- **Fixed Disks.** Fixed disks are permanent disks that cannot be removed. Data is archived off the disk onto another storage medium in order to free up space for new data.

Tape Storage

Tape storage is primarily used for archival storage. The recording medium is a thin polyester tape between 0.38cm and 2.54cm wide, about .025mm thick and coated with magnetic particles.

The tape is wound on wheels of various sizes. Data is recorded sequentially, one byte after the other, from the beginning of the tape to its end. Access times for tape storage are much slower than for floppy diskettes or hard disks. The following diagram shows how data is stored on the disk. The read/write head is comprised of several tracks, 9 tracks being very common. This means nine bits are recorded across the width of the tape simultaneously.

Using nine tracks, one byte of data plus a parity bit is recorded at a time (vertically). Characters are grouped together to form a record (often called a block). Each record is separated from the next record by a blank inter-record gap (IBG). A header field precedes each record. The IBG allows the software to position the tape for recording or playing at specific record numbers. Physical markers are used to indicate the ends of the tape and may be metallic foil, clear plastic or software markers encoded on the tape. Software encoding uses BOT (Beginning of Tape) and EOT (End of Tape) indicators.

Writing a groove in the reel (or notch tab in cartridge systems) provides protection. If the ring is fitted, this is detected when the reel is mounted on the tape drive. This then enables writing on the tape. Removal of the ring enables write protection.

Many operating systems and application programmes are still provided on tape systems, though CD-ROM is quickly replacing this.

Magnetic-Optical Disk Method

The magnetic-optical methods are based on the polarisation of the magnetic field where the polarisation is caused by heat. To be written, the block (sector) is heated to above 150 degree centigrade. Simultaneously a magnetic field approximately 10 times the strength of the earth's magnetic field is created. The individual dipoles in the material are then polarized according to this magnetic field. Hereby, a pit corresponds to a low value of the magnetic field. A land is coded through a high value of the magnetic field.

After the CD is irradiated with a laser beam, the polarisation of the light changes corresponding to the existing magnetisation. Using this process, the read operation is executed. For a delete activity, a constant magnetic field is created in the area of a block and the sector is simultaneously heated.

Video Disks

The video disk serves as the output of motion pictures and audio. The data are stored in an analog-coded format on the disk and the reproduced data meets the highest quality requirements. The motion picture on the video disk is encoded as frequency modulation and the audio signal is mixed with the video signal.

The main information of the mixed audio-video signal is the time at which the signal has the value zero. Hence, each zero cross-point corresponds to a change between a pit and a land on the disk. Such a change can occur at any time and is written to the disk in a non-quantised form, i.e., the pit length is not quantised. Therefore this method is time-continuous and analog.

The video disk was designed as Read Only Memory (ROM), since then many different write-once optical storage system have come out. These are known as Write Once Read Many (WORM) disk.

WORM (Write Once Read Many)

Write once optical storage media have a capacity between 600 MB and approximately 8 Gigabytes. The diametre of the disks is between 3.5 and 14 inches. The main advantage of WORM disk, compared to other mass storage media, is the ability to store large amount of data, which may not be changed later, i.e., an archive, which is safe. It can be written to once, though some CD writers support what is known as Multiple Sessions, which allows CD's to be written to more than once. In addition, for multiple session CD's, each session written has an overhead of approximately 20MB per session.

Optical Disks and Their Basic Technology

Optical disks use laser technology and special crystalline ceramics (amorphous crystal) to implement data storage. They are similar to an audio compact disk (CD). Optical disks for PC's store 660MB per disk. They have an access time of about 300ms (little slower than floppy). In principle, optical storage media use the intensity of the laser light as an information source. A laser beam of approximately 780 nm wavelength can be focused at approximately 1 micrometre. In a polycarbonate substrate layer there are holes, corresponding to the encoded data, which are called pits. The areas between these pits are called lands. The substrate layer is covered with a thin reflective layer. The laser beam is focused on the reflective layer from the substrate layer. The light is scattered by the pits and reflected by the lands. Therefore, the reflected beam has a strong intensity at the lands. The pits have depth of 0.12 um (from the substrate surface). The laser beam is lightly scattered at the pits, meaning it is reflected with a weak intensity. These two variations encode the binary 0's and 1's. A light sensitive diode picks up the reflected laser light from the surface of the disk and converts the light to digital data. Data is stored on a single spiral track. The rotational speed of the CD is altered so that the data on the track is always read at the same speed. This is called Constant Linear Velocity.

The compact disk chiefly consists of:

- The label
- The protective layer
- The reflective layer
- The substrate layer

In contrast to floppy disks and other conventional storage media, the entire optical disk information is stored in one track. Thus, the stored information can be easily played back at a continuous data rate. This has advantages for audio and video data as they are continuous data stream squares. Thc track is spiral. In case of a CD, the distance between the tracks is 1.6 um. The track width of each pit is 0.6 um. The pits have different lengths.

The main advantage of the optical disk in comparison to magnetic disks is that on the former 1.66 data bits per um can be stored. This results in a data density of 1,000,000 bits per mm square, which implies 16,000 tracks per inch. In comparison, a floppy disk has 96 tracks per inch.

While magnetisation can decrease over time and in case of tapes for example, crosstalk can occur, these effects are unknown in optical disks. Hence, this medium is very good for long time storage.

There are basically four main types of compact disc formats:

1. CD Audio
2. CD-ROM (Compact Disc-Read Only Memory)
3. CD-I (Compact Disc-Interactive)
4. CD-ROM/XA (CD-ROM Extended Architecture).

Compact Disk Digital Audio (CD-A)

The CD has a diametre of 12 cm, the disk is played at a Constant Linear Velocity (CLV). Therefore, the number of rotations per time unit depend on the particular radius of the accessed data. The spiral-shaped CD track consists of approximately 20,000 windings. In comparison an LP disk has only approximately 850 windings. The advantage of CD-DA is that it is not sensitive with respect to uncompressed audio to the usual appearance of reading errors. The disadvantage of the CD-DA technology is that its achieved reliability is too low for the storage of computer data. This leads to the further development of the CD technology.

Physical Standards

The physical standards for CD audio is popularly known as Red Book which is given as follows:

- Defined by Philips and Sony in 1980 and published in a red binder, hence Red Book.
- Standard needed so a CD made by any manufacturer can be read by any CD player.
- Physical block structure, 75 blocks are read per second, each block divided into 98 24 byte frames.
- Frames are encoded using EFM (Eight to Fourteen Modulation), CIRC (Cross Interleaved Reed Solomon Code) codes are inserted for error detection and correction.

Compact Disk-Read Only Memory (CD-ROM)

The Compact Disk-Read Only Memory (CD-ROM) was designed as the storage format for general computer data in addition to uncompressed audio data. Further, CD-ROM technology has been planned to be the basis for storage of other media (e.g., video). CD-ROM tracks are divided into audio and data types. One track itself may either contain audio only or data only. A CD-ROM can contain both types of tracks, tracks with audio and other tracks with data. In such a mixed form, the data tracks are usually located at the beginning of the CD- ROM and then followed by the audio tracks. Such a CD is called a Mixed Mode Disk.

A CD-ROM disc is a small plastic coated disc that holds information as tiny holes in a central metal layer. It looks and works like a normal audio CD. A laser beam is used to read the holes in the disc as it spins in the drive. To spin the disc and control the laser, a CD-ROM drive is required. Also a controller card is essential to interface the CD-ROM drive to PC. Some sound cards have a CD-ROM controller built in, otherwise a special card called SCSI (Small Computer System Interface) is needed.

CD-ROM drives can either be fitted inside PC in one of the free 5-1/4 inch drive bays in the front panel or can be fitted externally. External drives have their own case and power supply and are useful if there is need to share a drive between PCs but they still need a controller card in each PC.

At the front of all CD-ROM drives is an access slot for the disc. There are two ways of inserting the disc which vary according to the drive. Some manufacturers use a caddy. The disc is fitted inside the plastic caddy (which looks rather like a CD case) and then slide the whole lot inside the drive. Other drives use a tray like an audio CD player; a motorised tray slides out from the drive and the disc is placed on top and has to be pushed back into place.

Almost all CD-ROM drives can play audio CDs that can be listened to by plugging in a pair of headphones. User can control the play, stop and fast forward functions from the media player utility in Windows.

The features of the CD-ROM can be commonly stated as below:

- About 654.74 MB or 74.5 minutes of audio.
- One spiral groove with a few billion pits and lands.
- Written in CLV format (Constant Linear Velocity) opposed to CAV (Constant Angular Velocity).
- Can be gold (a CD-recordable disc) or silver (commercially replicated).

Single Speed/Double Speed/Quad Speed and Hex Speed CD-ROM – CD-ROM's first produced adhered to a set speed of 150KB/s. This is known as single speed CD-ROM. With the advent of multimedia and graphics, high speeds of data transfer are required. The following table lists the currently available speeds and data transfer rates for each.

Table 6.2 Speeds and Data Transfer Rates

Speed	Transfer Rate
x1	150KB/s
x2	300KB/s
x4	600KB/s
x8	1,200KB/s

Physical Standards

The physical standards for CD-ROM is popularly known as Yellow Book which is given as follows:

- Sony and Philips found that error rates on audio CDs were low, decided to use them for computer data.
- 1983 Yellow Standard for CD-ROM announced as an extension of the CD audio standard.
- An extra layer of error correction was added.
- Has 2 modes, mode 2 has less error correction and more data.

Mixed mode disc has both audio and CD-ROM block structure on different tracks.

CD-ROM Interfaces

CD-ROM's can be connected to a computer system using the following interfaces:

- SCSI
- IDE
- proprietary

The type of CD-ROM must have a matching controller type. For example, it is not possible to connect a SCSI CD-ROM using an IDE interface.

CD-I

CD-Interactive is a format that combines multimedia graphics, sound and video on a CD-ROM. It is especially designed for interactive use and is suited to presentations, trainings and games. Access to the information is controlled via a simple point and click menu interface, which people find easy to use and navigate. This explains its use in public type kiosks and sales presentations.

The compact disk interactive (CD-I) was developed by N V Philips and the Sony corporation prior to the specification of the CD-ROM/XA. In 1986, CD-I was announced and in 1988 was specified in the Green Book. CD-I was conceptually designed only for consumer electronics as an addition to a TV.

CD-I represents an entire system. It contains a CD-ROM based (not CD-ROM/XA) format with interleaving of different media and a definition of compression for different media. Further, CD-I defines a system software with CD-RTOS (Realtime Operating System), which is an OS-9 derivation with extensions for real-time processing and the output hardware for multimedia data.

The CD-I hardware is called the decoder. Its size is comparable with the size of a current VCR. It consists of a main processor from the Motorola 68,000 family and special video and audio elements. It also contains the CD player with a controller, joystick and mouse interface. Besides this interface, an interface to an RGB monitor or TV is planned. CD-I devices are considered to be a replacement and/or extension of the CD-DA devices in the consumer environment.

All CD formats are based on the same CD-DA standard but it is not always possible to play a CD-I disk on CD-DA device. It is also not correct to assume that CD-I devices will replace all CD-DA devices, for example. Therefore, there is a need for a format specification of an optical disk which can be played by CD-DA devices as well as CD-I devices – namely the Compact Disk Interactive Ready Format.

Physical Standards

The physical standards for CD-I is known as Green Book Standard and are listed as below:

- Announced in 1986 to help with synchronisation of audio and data tracks.
- CD-I (Compact Disc-Interactive) built on the CD-ROM mode 2 block structure and interleaves audio and data. Also has 2 modes, mode 1 with additional EDC/ECC codes, mode 2 without.

Photo CD

Introduced in 1992, the Photo CD is a CD-ROM. The photo compact disk from Eastman Kodak and N V Philips company is an example of a CD bridge disk. Here, photographs of a high quality are stored. The photo CD is based on the mechanism of "Write Once" characteristics. It can be read as a CD bridge disk from CD-I and CD-ROM/XA devices. Additionally, it can be read and written as CD-WO on special Photo-CD devices.

Photo-CD holds up to 100 high-resolution images that are (2048 × 3072 pixels) captured from 35mm film. A photo CD master disc stores images up to five different levels of resolution, from small thumbnail sizes of 128 × 192 pixels to 2048 × 3072 pixels. This is 16 times larger than standard TV resolutions and four times the resolution currently being considered for HDTV (High Definition TV).

Users can take their negatives to a Kodak licensed photo processing shop and have their pictures transferred onto photo CD. Most CD-ROM drives sold in personal computers are photo CD compatible. The entire Photo CD does not need to be filled at once, photos can be added onto the photo CD as required.

Physical Standards

The physical standards for Photo CD are mentioned as given on the page in the Orange Book alongwith recordable compact disc standard for both M-O and W-O.

- Announced in 1990 to address the new recordable optical media and provide specifications for incremental writes.
- Divided into 2 parts, Compact Disc-Magneto Optical (CD-MO) and Compact Disc-Write Once (CD-WO).
- Covers Multi-session discs, such as the Kodak Photo CD.

CD-ROM Extended Architecture (CD-ROM/XA)

N V Philips, Sony and Microsoft Corporation established the CD-ROM/Extended (CD-ROM/XA) standard. The main motivation for this additional development was the concurrent output of several media which was not sufficiently covered in the previous approaches.

CD-ROM/XA allows interleaved storage of different media. Audio can be compressed in different quality levels with Adaptive Differential Pulse Code Modulation (ADPCM). This compression improves the entire CD-DA duration from 74 uncompressed CD-DA minutes to over 19 hours of lower quality audio by reducing the audio signal to four bits per sample. Further, this compression is necessary for simultaneous retrieval of other media. MPEG audio does not use ADPCM coding and therefore is not compatible with the CD-ROM/XA specification.

Data Standards

The data standards for optical storage media can be described as below.

The ISO 9660 Format

The ISO 9660 data interchange format, adopted in 1987 and widely used is an accepted computer industry standard. UNIX, Macintosh and DOS machines can read CDs mastered in this format. The IS0 9660 level 1 places limits on the directory and file structure that can be placed on the CD-ROM. Level 1 ISO-9660 defines names to be the familiar 8+3 convention. The eight characters are for the name, a period, followed by three characters for the file type, all in upper case. Many special characters (space, hyphen, tilde, equals and plus) are forbidden. There is also a file version number, separated from the name by a semicolon, but it is often ignored.

Level 2 ISO-9660 allows longer filenames and deeper directory structures (32 levels instead of 8), but is not usable on some systems, notably MS-DOS.

Rock Ridge

The Rock Ridge extensions to ISO-9660 define a way for UNIX like long mixed-case filenames and symbolic links to be supported. This uses the System Use Area and Application Use Area in the ISO 9660 directory record to store Unix file. Because it is still an ISO-9660 file system, machines can still read the files that do not support Rock Ridge. They just won't see the long forms of the names. UNIX systems and the Macintosh support Rock Ridge. DOS and Windows currently don't support it.

HFS (Hierarchical File System)

HFS is the Hierarchical File System, used by the Macintosh. This is used in place of the ISO-9660 file system, making the disc unusable on systems that do not support HFS. At present, the only systems that can read HFS CD-ROMS are Macintosh, Amigas and the Apple IIgs and SGI machines running Irix (they appear as AppleDouble format).

Joliet

Microsoft created its own standard called Joliet. Win95 and WinNT currently support this. It is useful when doing backups from Win95 onto a CD-R, because the disc is still readable as ISO-9660 but shows the long filenames under Win95.

Review Questions

1. Discuss various storage devices.
2. Explain the characteristics and terminology used for various storage devices.
3. Compare storage devices using various criterias.
4. Describe the operation of storage devices.
5. Define data standards for optical storage media.
6. What is CD-ROM? Compare various optical storage media.

CHAPTER VII

Multimedia Networking

1. *Introduction*.. 115
2. *Transmission Media*... 116
3. *Networking Concepts and Terms*...................... 125
4. *Local Area Network (LAN) Technologies*......... 128
5. *Wide Area Network (WAN)*............................... 135

CHAPTER 7

Multimedia Networking

Introduction

Multimedia can be roughly defined as a technology that enables humans to use computers capable of processing textual data, audio and video, still pictures and animation. Applications range over entertainment, education, information provision, design, video conferencing, application sharing, remote working and virtual reality experiences.

In the beginning, multimedia applications for computers were developed for single computing platforms such as the PC, Apple Macintosh and games machines. The importance of networking for multimedia was realised with the development of communication technology. Therefore, networking capabilities of multimedia computers is generating new applications. This is providing gains in efficiency, cost and use when multimedia resources are part of distributed computing systems. Widening of access to multimedia sources and potential markets in multimedia, video and information are a commercial driving force for networking multimedia.

The need of networking multimedia lies in the fact that the characteristics of multimedia make substantial demands on storage and transmission systems. Data compression for audio, video and images can be used to reduce the above demands of multimedia but usually at the expense of some loss in the detail compared with the source and at extra cost. The ways in which users in multimedia sessions connect with others is largely dependent upon the storage and transmission systems in use. For example, in education multimedia, learning packages have been mounted on file-servers, use of the world wide web is widespread and some video conferencing is being used. These require some kind of transmission and storage media and therefore networking of computer based multimedia is possible. The information, which has previously been presented, on radio, TV, or in books, is now being presented or can be accessed by computer networks.

Transmission Media

There are various ways to transmit the multimedia data. These categories can be broadly divided into guided and unguided media. The data is encoded and then energy is transmitted. Similarly at the receiving end the energy is decoded back to data. This energy can be electrical, light, radio, etc. This transmitted energy is carried through some sort of medium. Each form of energy has different properties and requirements for transmission. Transmitter encodes data as energy and transmits energy through the medium. This requires special hardware for data encoding and connection to transmission medium. Media can be copper, glass, air, etc. These techniques have been briefly discussed below.

Copper Conductors

Copper conductors are in the form of a twisted pair which uses two wires and are popular for telephone networks. The energy flow is in guided media. Copper wire is a mature technology, rugged and inexpensive. The maximum transmission speed is limited in this case. The copper conductor that carries analogue data can be used to carry digital data also in association with Modem. Modem is a device used to convert digital signal into analog signal and *vice versa*. The data rate in this category is limited to around 28 Kbps. The introduction of the Integrated Services Digital Network (ISDN) led to the use of improved modulation and coding schemes and data rate up to 128 Kbps. Local Area Networks (LANs) also use copper cable twisted pairs. These networks have also been upgraded to provide support for high bit rate real time multimedia. A recent development is Asymmetric Digital Subscriber Lines (ADSL) technology which is aimed at using two wire copper loops at data rates of 1.544 Mbps in the network to user direction and about 600 Kbps from the user to network.

Figure 7.1 Two wire copper conductor

The twisted pair cable may be defined in two categories based upon shielding and without shielding:

Unshielded Twisted Pair (UTP)

UTP as depicted in Figure 7.2 is the copper media, inherited from telephony, which is being used for increasingly higher data rates and is rapidly becoming the de facto standard for horizontal wiring. Horizontal wiring specifies the connection between and including, the outlet and the termination in the communication closet. The horizontal is limited to a maximum of 90 μετρες. This is independent of the media type so that the communication closet is common to all media and all applications operating over the media. In addition, there is an allowance for 3 metres in the work area and 6 metres for cross connecting in the closet for a total of 99 metres.

The recommended media and connectors for the horizontal are as follow:

- 100-ohm unshielded twisted pair - 4 pairs, 8-pin modular connector (ISDN).
- 150-ohm shielded twisted pair - 2 pairs (IBM connector or RJ45).
- 50-ohm coax (thin) - IEEE 10BASE2, standard BNC connector.
- 62.5/125 multi mode fibre.

A UTP cable contains from 2 to 4,200 twisted pairs. The advantages of UTP is the flexibility, low cost media and can be used for either voice or data communications. Its greatest disadvantage is the limited bandwidth, which restricts long distance transmission with low error rates.

Figure 7.2 Unshielded Twisted Pair (UTP)

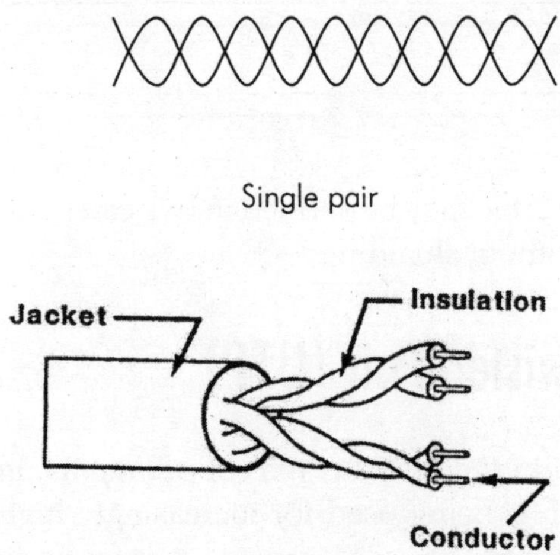

Shielded Copper

Shielded twisted pair (STP) differs from UTP in that a metallic shield or screen surrounds the pairs, which may or may not be twisted. As illustrated in Figure 7.3, the pairs can be individually shielded. A single shield can surround a cable containing multiple pairs or both techniques can be employed in tandem. The shield itself is made of aluminium, steel, or copper; is in the form of a metallic foil or woven meshes; and is electrically grounded. Although less effective, the shield sometimes is in the form of nickel and/or gold plating of the individual conductors.

Figure 7.3 Shielded Twisted Pair (STP) configuration

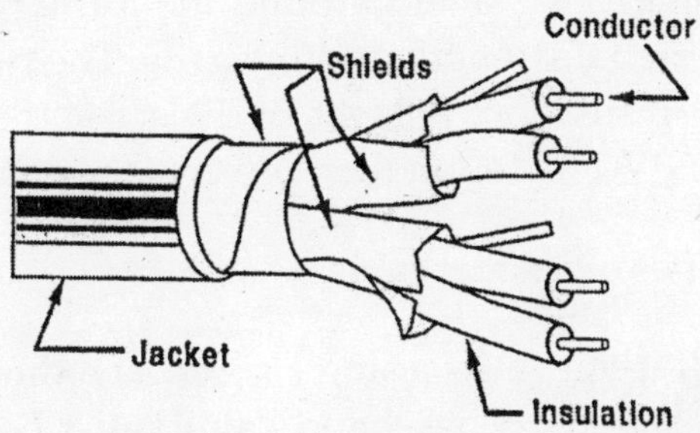

Shielded copper offers the advantage of enhanced performance for reasons of reduced emissions and reduction of electromagnetic interference. Reduction of emissions offers the advantage of maintaining the strength of the signal through the confinement of the electromagnetic field within the conductor; in other words, signal loss is reduced. An additional benefit of this reduction of emissions is that high-frequency signals do not cause interference in adjacent pairs or cables. Immunity from interference is realized through the shielding process, which reflects electromagnetic noise from outside sources, such as electric motors, other cables and wires and radio systems.

Shielded twisted pair, on the other hand, has several disadvantages. First, the raw cost of acquisition is greater as the medium is more expensive to produce. Second, the cost of deployment is greater as the additional weight of the shield makes it more difficult to deploy. Additionally, the electrical grounding of the shield requires more time and effort.

Coaxial Cable

Coaxial cable is a guided media and still an effective medium to use in multimedia. Coaxial cable includes shield for improved performance and therefore is expensive. Cable TV networks use coaxial cables. Local area networks can operate over coaxial cable to the 10BASE5, 10BASE2 and 10BASET specification. In general coaxial cable enables longer distance transmission at higher data rates than twisted pair cable, but is more expensive.

Coaxial Cable as shown in Figure 7.4 is a very robust shielded copper wire two-conductor cable in which solid centre conductor running concentrically (coaxial) inside a solid outer circular conductor. This forms an electromagnetic shield around the former that serves to greatly improve signal strength and integrity. The two conductors are separated by insulation. A layer of dielectric (nonconductive) material, such as PVC or Teflon then protects the entire cable.

There are two types of coaxial cables:

- **Baseband.** It transmits a single signal at a time at very high speed. The signal on baseband cable must be amplified at specified distances. It is used for local area networks.
- **Broadband.** It can transmit many simultaneous signals using different frequencies.

Figure 7.4 Coaxial Cable Configuration

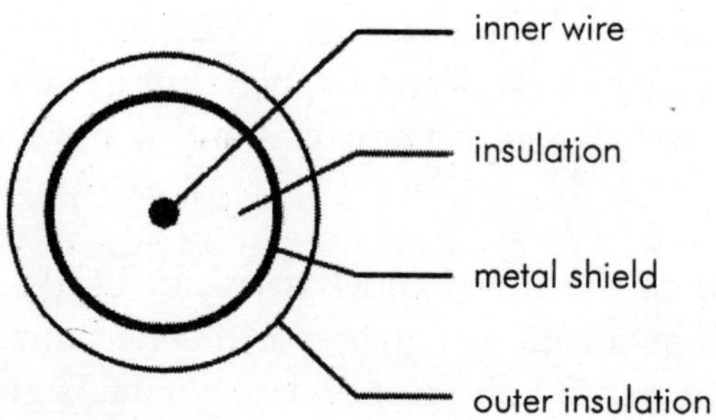

Optical Fibre

The geometry of coaxial cable significantly reduces the various limiting effects, the maximum signal frequency and hence the information rate that can be transmitted using a solid conductor, although very high, is limited. This is also the case for twisted lines. Optical fibre differs from both these transmission media in that it carries the transmitted information in the form of a fluctuating beam of light in a glass fibre rather than as an electrical signal on a wire.

Optical fibre transmission has become a strong support for digital network owing to its high capacity and other factors favourable for digital communication on which the multimedia network will depend. Thin glass fibre that is very clear and designed to reflect light internally for efficient transmission carries light with encoded data. Plastic jacket allows fibre to bend (some!) without breaking. Light Emitting Diode (LED) or laser injects light into fibre for transmission. Light sensitive receiver at the other end translates light back into data.

On campus, the provision of optical fibre enables the creation of high capacity backbones to local area networks. In principle, optical fibre can carry almost any type of traffic, at high data rates. It should be noted that there are different types of optical fibres – single mode, multi mode, with different sizes and attenuation characteristics. When upgrading from one technology to another, for example, FDDI to ATM, this may become important.

Fibre optic transmission systems are opto-electric in nature. In other words, a combination of optical and electrical electromagnetic energy is involved. The signal originates as an electrical signal, which is translated into an optical signal, which subsequently is reconverted into an electrical signal at the receiving end.

The optical fibre consists of three parts. This is shown in Figure 7.4:

- CORE - made of glass
- CLADDING - made of glass with lower refractive index
- Plastic coating

The light pulse travels down the centre core of the glass fibre. Surrounding the inner core is a layer of glass cladding, with a slightly different refractive index. The cladding serves to reflect the light waves back into the inner core. Surrounding the cladding is a layer of protective plastic coating that seals the cable and provides mechanical protection. Typically, multiple fibres are housed in a single sheath, which may be heavily armored.

Figure 7.5 Glass fibre optic cable – side view and cross section

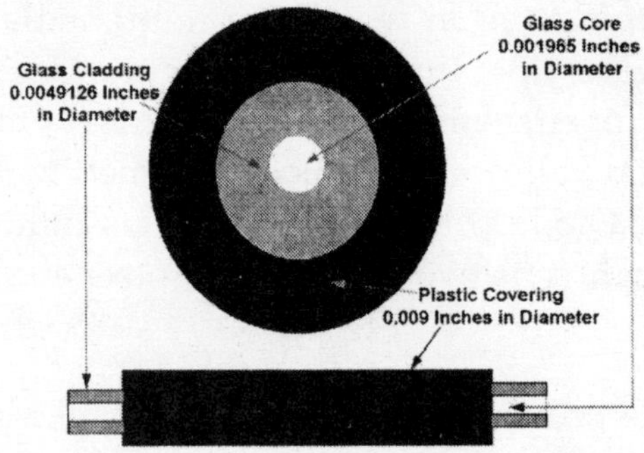

Light propagates along the optical fibre core in one of three ways as given below depending on the type and width of core material used.

- **Step Index Multimode Fibre.** Multimode fibre is less expensive to produce and inferior in performance because of the larger diaμετρε of the inner core. When the light rays travel down the fibre, they spread out due to a phenomenon known as modal dispersion. Although reflected back into the inner core by the cladding, they travel different distances and, therefore, arrive at different times. The received signal, thus, has a wider pulse width than the input signal with a corresponding decrease in the speed of transmission. As a result, multimode fibre is relegated to applications involving relatively short distances and lower speeds of transmission, for example, LANs and campus environments.

- **Graded Index Multimode Fibre.** Dispersion can be reduced using a core material that has a variable refractive index. In such multimode graded index fibre light is refracted by an increasing amount as it moves away from the core. This has the effect of narrowing the pulse width of the received signal compared with stepped index fibre, allowing a corresponding increase in the speed of transmission.

- **Monomode/Singlemode fibre.** This has a thinner inner core; therefore, it performs better than does multimode fibre over longer distances at higher transmission rates. Due to reduced core diaμετρε all the emitted light propagates along a single path. Consequently the received signal is of a comparable width to the input signal. Although more costly, monomode fibre is used to advantage in long haul and especially in high bandwidth applications.

Advantages of optical fibres may be listed as:

- Immunity to electromagnetic interference and crosstalk
- No electrical ground loop or short circuit problems
- Small size and light-weight
- Large bandwidth for size and weight
- Safe in combustible areas (no arching)
- Immunity to lightning and electrical discharges
- Longer cable runs between repeaters
- Flexibility and high strength
- Potential high temperature operation
- Secure against signal leakage and interference
- No electrical hazard when cut or damaged.

Radio Systems

Radio systems have a great impact on multimedia. In this case, data are transmitted using radio waves. Energy travels through the air rather than copper or glass. There are different techniques to convert the data suitable for this mode of communication. Conceptually similar to radio, TV and cellular phones, radio waves can travel through walls and through an entire building. They can travel for long distances using satellite communication or short distance using wireless communication.

Use of this technology for delivery of real time multimedia material should be treated carefully because radio links are susceptible to fading, interference, random delays, etc. For non-real time use, this technology is likely to perform as well as current Ethernet LANs.

Microwave radio is a form of radio transmission that uses ultra-high frequencies. There are several frequency ranges assigned to microwave systems, all of which are in the GHz range and the wavelength in the millimetre range. This very short wavelength gives rise to the term microwave. Such high frequency signals are especially susceptible to attenuation and, therefore must be amplified or repeated after a particular distance.

In order to maximize the strength of such a high frequency signal and, therefore, to increase the distance of transmission at acceptable levels, the radio beams are highly focused. The transmit antenna is centred in a concave, reflective metal dish which serves to focus the radio beam with maximum effect on the receiving antenna, as illustrated in Figure 7.6. The receiving antenna, similarly, is centred in a concave metal dish, which serves to collect the maximum amount of incoming signal.

Figure 7.6 Point-to-point microwave

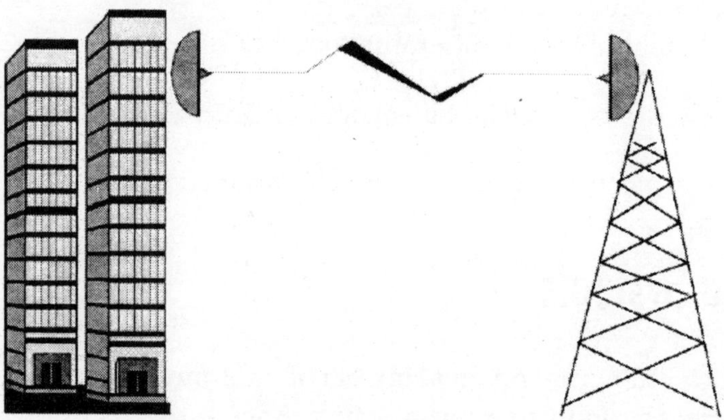

It is a point-to-point, rather than a broadcast, transmission system. Additionally, each antenna must be within line of sight of the next antenna. Given the curvature of the earth and the obvious problems of transmitting through it, microwave hops generally are limited to 50 miles (80 km). If the frequencies are higher within the microwave band given in Table 7.1, this impact is more than lower frequencies in the same band.

Table 7.1 Microwave frequency bands

Frequency Bands	Maximum Antenna Separation	Analog/Digital
4–6 GHz	32-48 Km	Analog
10-12 GHz	16-24 Km	Digital
18-23 GHz	8-11 Km	Digital

Networking Concepts and Terms

A network is a two or more computer interconnection, in a peer to peer or client to server fashion, most often over a shared and often virtual connection. This is in direct contrast to the old terminal to host hardwired connection. A network can still support terminal to host connections via terminal emulators or terminal servers but provides much greater flexibility in switching connections.

Following are some major reasons to implement the network:

- Sharing of resources can be done easily
- Reliability-There is no central computer so if one breaks down we can use others
- Networks allow us to be mobile.

A network is accomplished using three basic components:

- Hardware
- Protocols (software)
- Applications (useful software).

Each of these is actually comprised of several layers. The concept of layers is very important to networking and computer designs as well. Each layer protects the layer above from the layer below so that one layer can change with minimum impact on the upper layers. In some cases, this protection is so good that an application may not know that it is running on a different hardware. The OSI network model defines seven layers that can be grouped into three broad categories:

- Hardware
- Protocols
- Applications

Network Architecture and OSI

- **Open System.** While computer networks have existed for sometime, proprietary networks from different suppliers could not be used to inter-communicate. The open systems concept was developed to solve this compatibility problem. An open system is built using widely accepted standards. Open systems allow end users to select equipment from a number of suppliers to realise an optimal solution for their applications.
- **The ISO Model.** The International Standard Organization (ISO), in an effort to encourage 'open' networks, developed an open systems interconnect reference model. The model logically groups the functions and sets rules, called protocols, necessary to establish and conduct communication between two or more parties. The model consists of seven functions, often referred to as layers as shown in Figure 7.7.

Figure 7.7 Seven-Layer Model

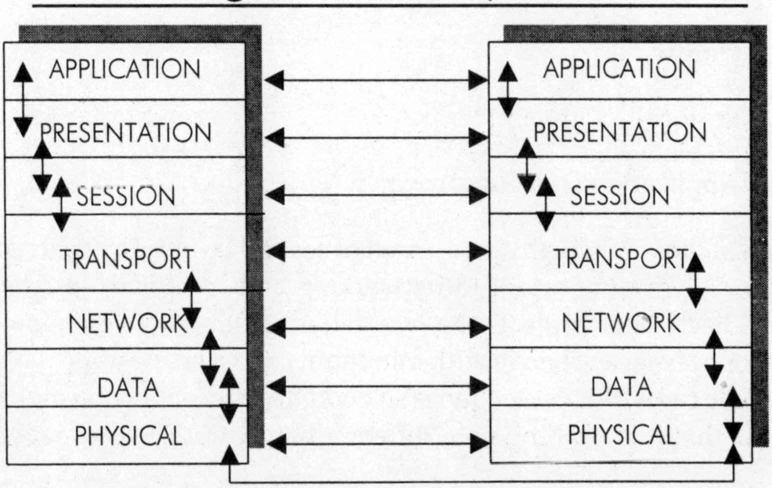

Layers and their Functions

- **Physical Layer.** It describes the physical media over which the bit stream is to be as also the electrical and mechanical aspects of interfacing to a physical medium for transmitting data, as well as setting up, maintaining and disconnecting physical links. It is primarily concerned with moving bits from one node to the next over the physical link.

- **Data Link Layer.** It takes the bits that are received by the physical layer and detects errors. This establishes an error-free communications path between network nodes over the physical channel, frames messages for transmission, checks integrity of received messages, manages access to and use of the channel, ensures proper sequence of transmitted data.

- **Network Layer.** In addition to routing, this layer is responsible for establishing and maintaining the connection.

- **Transport Layer.** This layer divides up a transmitting message into packets and reassembles them at the receiving end.

The next three layers are applications oriented and have to do with the operations performed by the user rather than with the network.

- **Session Layer.** The session layer manages logging in and logging off procedures. It manages dialogues between two users/applications.

- **Presentation Layer.** Responsible for converting file record formats. Performs conversion between ASCII and EBCDIC character codes, does data compression and encrypts data if necessary.

- **Application Layer.** Determines how the user is using the data network. It allows user to use the network. For example, it provides network (NW) based services to the end user. Examples of NW services are distributed databases, electronic mail, resource sharing, file transfers, remote file access and network management. This layer defines the nature of the task or application to be performed.

The last three layers are thus mainly concerned with the organisation of terminal software and are not directly the concern of communications engineers. The transport layer is the one which links the communication processes to these software oriented protocols.

The basic philosophy of the 7-layer model is that each layer may be defined independent of every other layer. Thus, from the user point of view, interchange takes effect across each operation and passes down through the layers of the model until data interchange is affected through the physical connection.

Local Area Network (LAN) Technologies

Local Area Networks (LANs) are most often described as privately owned networks that offer reliable high speed communication channels optimized for connecting information processing equipment in a limited geographical area, namely, an office, building, complex of buildings, or campus.

LANs, in addition to linking the computer equipment available in particular premises, can also provide a connection to other networks, either through a computer which is attached to both networks, or through a dedicated device called a Gateway. The main users of LANs include business organisations, research and development groups in science and engineering, industry and educational institutions. The electronic or paperless office concept is possible with LANs.

The chief advantages of LANs can be witnessed in the sharing of resources. Resources could be information: (1) Data Files (2) E-mail (3) Voice Mail (4) Software (5) Hardware (Hard disk, printer, fax etc.).

Disadvantages of LANs mainly relate to security of files and accounts.

LAN Topologies

LANs are classified depending on the topology, access methods, signalling methods, transmission medium and transmission mode.

The control of the network is of two types – centralized and distributed. With centralized control, access to the network and allocation of channel is controlled by one node, such as a dedicated communications processor or switch. When control is distributed, nodes have the ability to establish connections and access the network channel independently, according to an accepted set of rules.

Most LANs are based on simple structured topologies, like the ring, bus or star. Some of the basic characteristics of these topologies are outlined below:

- **Star Networks.** The distinguishing feature of star topology is that all nodes are joined at a single point as shown in Figure 7.8 (a). Star topology is frequently used for networks in which control of the network is located in the central node. This method is optimal when the bulk of communication is between the central and outlying nodes. If traffic is high between outlying nodes, an undue switching burden is placed on the central node.

Figure 7.8 (a) Star Topology

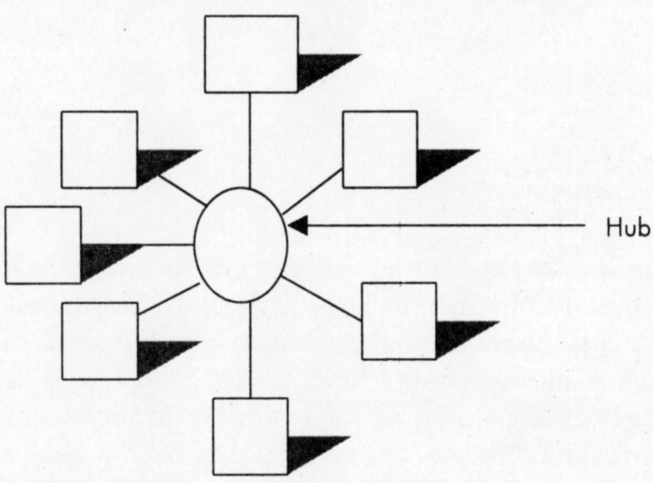

- **Ring Networks.** The ring architecture is a distributed architecture, with minimal connectivity and a topology of two links connected to every node and forms unbroken circular configuration as shown in Figure 7.8 (b). Transmitted messages travel from node to node around the ring. Each node must be able to recognize its own address in order to accept messages. In addition, each node serves as an active repeater, re-transmitting messages of other nodes. Ring networks with centralized control are known as Loops. When ring networks with distributed control are used, some form of control strategies must be used to avoid conflicting demands for the shared channel. The popular control strategies are token passing, circulating slot, register insertion techniques. If any node in ring fails, the communication through ring will be lost. To avoid such situation, an extra ring parallel to the existing ring is used in case of failure.

Figure 7.8 (b) Ring Topology with single and dual ring

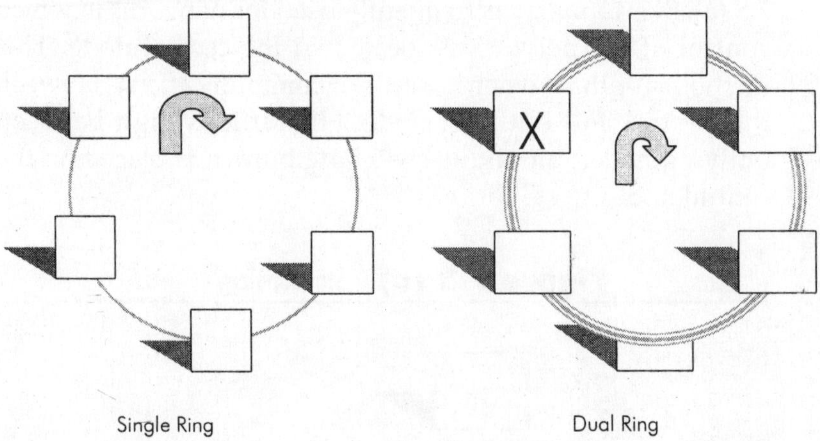

X: Failure of the computer

- **Bus Networks.** The bus topology as shown in Figure 7.8 (c) is employed frequently in the LANs with distributed control. In this all nodes share the common bus. Messages placed on the bus are transmitted to all nodes. Nodes must be able to recognize their own address in order to receive messages. However, unlike nodes in a ring, they do not have to repeat and forward massages intended for other nodes. As a result there is none of the delay and overhead associated with re-transmitting messages at each intervening node. Because of the passive role the nods play in transmission on the bus, network operation will continue in the event of node failures. This makes distributed BUS network's inherently resistive to single point failures.

Figure 7.8 (c) Bus Topology

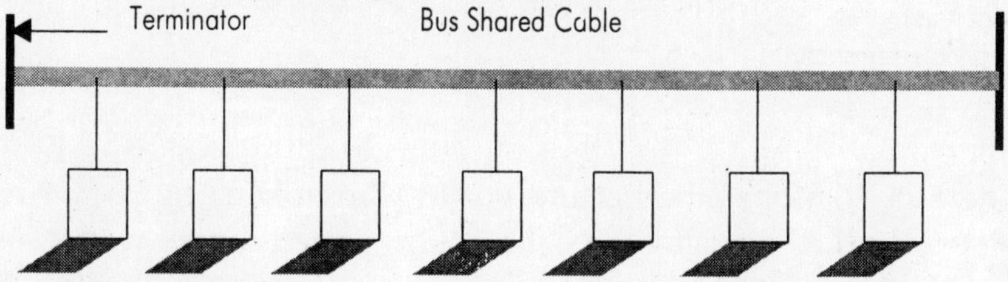

LAN Standards

The three standard protocols for LAN for multimedia applications are Ethernet, Fast Ethernet, Fibre Distributed Data Interface (FDDI). There are some more standards like iso-ethernet, proprietary LAN and Local ATM. These are still under development stage and discussions of these are beyond the scope of this book.

Ethernet

Ethernet as shown in Figure 7.9 was one of the first LAN architectures. The standard provides high speed transmission at an economical price, offering a broad base support for a variety of LAN and micro-to-mainframe applications. An Ethernet cable comes in several types. The maximum length of your LAN segment is determined by which type you choose or which types you intermix. There is twisted pair, thin coaxial and thick coaxial Ethernet cables. Each of these is rated at 10Mbit per second (Mbps). The speed between nodes is determined by how many nodes are trying to communicate at any given time. The thick coaxial was the first used.

Figure 7.9 Ethernet

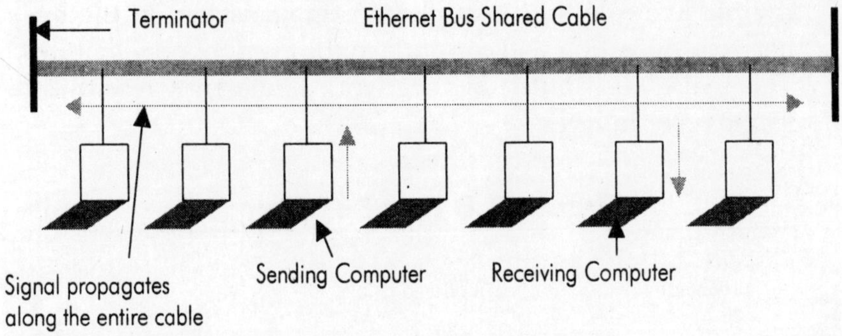

There are 10 Mbps Ethernet and 4 or 16 Mbps token ring Local Area Networks (LANs) using coaxial cable or twisted copper wire. Most new LANs use twisted copper wire cable. Thin coaxial comes in two types. Because of lower cost and ease of installation, thin coaxial is often called cheaper net. It has a shorter overall maximum length than thickness. There are adapters to go between thick and thin but the overall length can be reduced to that of thin. There are devices called hubs which may not reduce the limit and can provide conversion between one cable type to another. Multimedia file servers can be attached to such LANs. Both Novell and Microsoft have developed software to support video on these traditional LANs.

Twisted pair is the current rage because it can be used for other things as well, such as voice. Ethernet over twisted pair is called 10BaseT and is most often configured as a star with an Ethernet switch at the centre usually in a wiring closet. The switch allows for the longer length required for a star configuration. Using a switch provides a lot of other benefits and options such as diagnostic tools and functions for monitoring the health of the LAN segment. It also provides improved performance by dividing LAN segments up into segments with only a few attached users. Switched Ethernet takes this approach to the limit by enabling only one user to access a single segment that is then connected to a higher capacity network at a central hub by a switch. The use of a switch permits the filtering of packets based on address. Switching times need to be fast enough to deliver packets at the basic 10 Mbps Ethernet line rate. An Ethernet switch would be equipped with a higher speed ATM or FDDI interface to other networks. However, even with one user per

Ethernet switch port or segment contention between different applications on the same machine or incoming and outgoing traffic can occur.

Fast Ethernet

A new version is Fast Ethernet that also runs at 100 Mbps but unlike FDDI it can coexist on the same wire as regular Ethernet. They even make hybrid cards that can do both 10 and 100 Mbps depending on what the host they are talking to can support. The IEEE has set out the aims of the 100 Mbps Ethernet LAN standard as follows:

- Line Rate of 100 Mbps
- 100 metre distances permissible to the Ethernet hub
- Category 3 to 5 twisted pair operation
- Equivalent error rates to 10 Mbps
- Compliance with electromagnetic compatibility standards
- Simultaneous support of 10 Mbps and 100 Mbps
- Use of RJ-45 connector.

Most of the 10 Mbps paraμετρες including the CSMA/CD media access protocol will remain unchanged and the standard is being named 100Base-T. Another 100 Mbps standard called 100VG-AnyLAN has also been proposed and changes the media access protocol to a demand priority system. Fast Ethernet products are only just starting to appear. Use of both standards will require a change out of workstation and hub cards.

FDDI

Several grades of twisted pair wire exist. The best class can also carry FDDI (Fibre Distributed Data Interface), which is new high speed token ring style network architecture. FDDI can handle speeds of 100 Mbps. FDDI is usually carried over fibre optic cable for long distances. There is also Gigabit per second network architectures for short distance applications such as a cluster of computer servers.

One reason FDDI came into being is that Ethernet performance degrades rapidly as the capacity of the bandwidth is approached. This means that the number of nodes that a LAN segment can support is limited. Depending on the activity level of the nodes, as many as 100 nodes can be supported on a LAN segment. Beyond that you should consider subdividing into multiple LAN segments with bridges and routers.

The FDDI was the only standards based technology operating at 100 Mbps for some time. Logically FDDI consists of a dual ring but it may be implemented as a physical star. Key feature of FDDI include:

- Shared medium based on a token passing medium access control
- Compatibility with IEEE 802 LANs
- Ability to use a wide range of physical medium including multi mode fibre, single mode fibre, shield and unshielded twisted pair

Figure 7.10 FDDI with single and dual ring

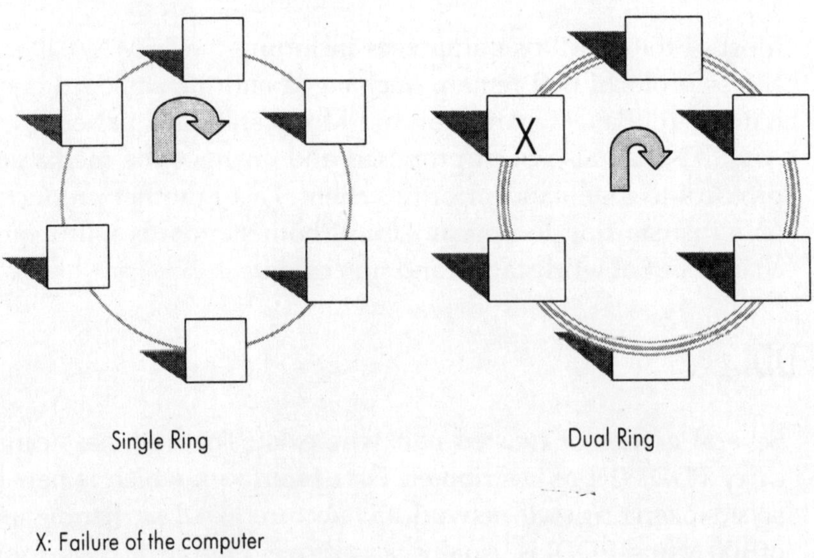

- Operation at 100 Mbps
- Support for 500 workstations
- Maximum fibre length of 200 Km
- Ability to allocate bandwidth dynamically so that both synchronous and asynchronous services can be provided.

Wide Area Network (WAN) Services

LANs can be extended to a wider area but it cannot be extended arbitrarily far or to handle arbitrarily many computers. There is a distance limitation even with extensions. Therefore, other technologies for larger networks are needed. The networks can be broadly divided into three categories namely:

- LAN for a single building,
- Metropolitan Area Network (MAN) - single city and
- WAN - country, continent and planet.

WAN is composed of a number of autonomous computer that are distributed over a large geographical area as shown in Figure 7.11. LAN can be extended across large distances using Satellite Bridge but still this cannot accommodate many computers arbitrarily. WAN must be scalable to long distances and many computers. Therefore, network must replace shared medium with packet switches to span long distances or many computers. Each switch moves an entire packet from one connection to another. This mechanism is called packet switching. These switches are nothing but a small computer with network interfaces, memory and program dedicated to packet switching function. These Packet switches may connect to computers and to other packet switches, typically high speed connections to other packets switches, lower speed to computers as shown in Figure 7.11. These Packet switches can be linked together to form WANs. WANs need not be symmetric or have regular connections, i.e., each switch may connect to one or more other switches and one or more computers.

Figure 7.11 Packet switches as building blocks to make a WAN

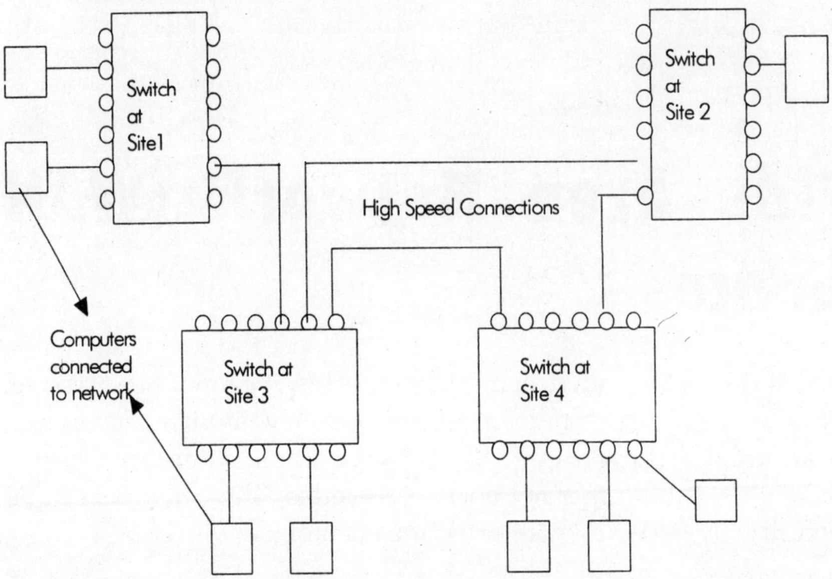

Data delivery from one computer to another is accomplished through store-and-forward technology. Packet switch stores incoming packet and forwards the packet to another switch or computer that has internal memory. Therefore this can hold packet in queue if outgoing connection is busy.

WAN Technologies

ARPANET

This may be considered as the breakthrough for many of the current ideas, algorithms and Internet technologies. It started in 1960s and was funded by Advanced Research Projects Agency, an organization of the US Defence Department.

X.25

X.25 is considered as an early standard for connection-oriented networking from ITU, which was originally CCITT. Earlier, it was developed for computer connections, used for terminal/timesharing connection.

X.25 defines the protocols from layer 1 (physical layer) to layer 3 (network layer) as shown in Figure 7.12. When X.25 is used the user can select any protocol for layer 4 or higher.

Figure 7.12 X.25 and OSI reference Model

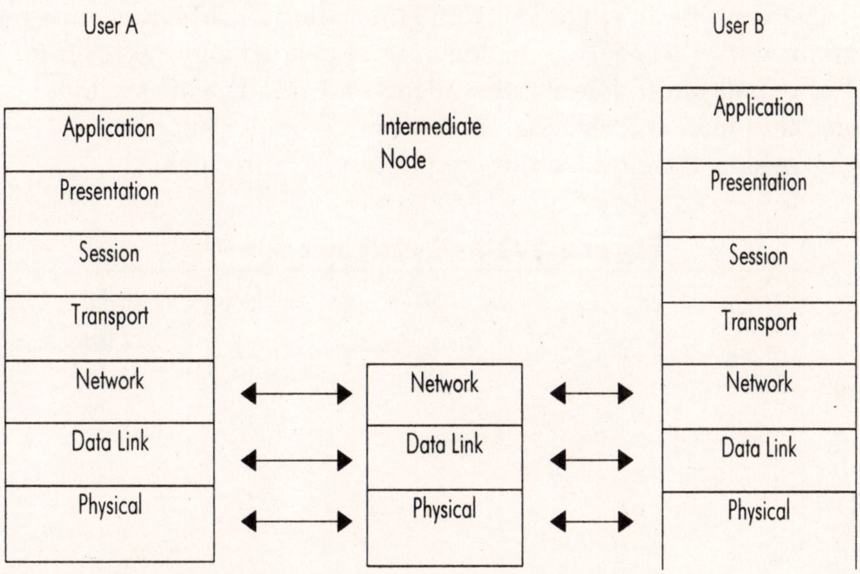

Characteristics of X.25

In addition to the characteristics of the packet switched network, X.25 has the following characteristics:

- Multiple logical channels can be set on a single physical line.
- Terminals of different communication speeds can communicate.
- The procedure for transmission controls can be changed.

Integrated Services Digital Network (ISDN)

In the real world the delivery of multimedia requires a widespread network capable of delivering at high data rates. The current implementation of ISDN in the narrow band form is the best access and delivery medium available. It has called integrated because it works with the well-known analog voice telephone network. This integrates various services like telephone, facsimile, picture, data and telex, etc., as shown in Figure 7.13. ISDN offers point to point delivery, network access and network interconnection for multimedia. Different data rates from 64 Kbps up to 2 Mbps are commercially available which can meet many needs for multimedia. The data rate of ISDN is 64 KBPS as compared to about 33.6 KBPS available with ordinary analog voice lines. The 64 KBPS data rate for ISDN is typical, while 33.6 KBPS for analog voice is rarely ever sustained in practice. Two channels can be bonded together to offer 128kbps data rates. Note also that all these are raw data rates without compression, if the terminal adapter or computer supports data compression, the effective throughput can be much higher.

Figure 7.13 Network Using ISDN

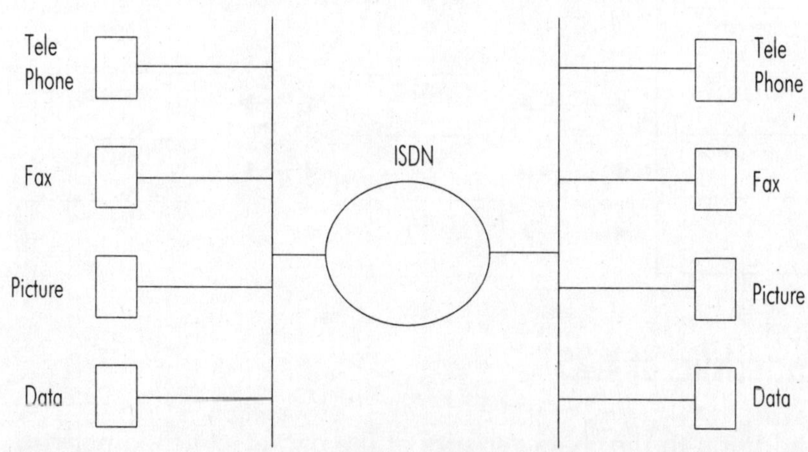

ISDN lines are much faster and of higher quality than analog voice grade lines. The digital ISDN line is virtually error free but the analog modem will usually experience significant data errors during the transfer. While the data errors will be detected and corrected by the equipment and software, the errors will slow the transfer of data over analog modems even further. The most noticeable benefit of

ISDN speeds is observed when using interactive Internet applications like world wide web browsers. ISDN speeds also make acceptable quality real-time video and audio over the Internet a reality.

ISDN is accessed through one of two services, named by the CCITT as Basic Rate Interface (BRI) and Primary Rate Interface (PRI). BRI provides 144Kbps using the existing twisted pair copper telephone cable.

BRI includes 2 B channels and 1 D channels. This may be written as 2B+D. B channel (Bearer) provides 64Kbps data transmission and can carry voice or data. D channel (Delta) operates at 16Kbps and is used for control, i.e., for signalling between user devices and the ISDN. Therefore, the total data rate of BRA is 144 Kbps audio digitized using pulse code modulation (PCM).

PRI can carry 30 independent voice or data channels, each at 64 Kbps. The structure has a 64 Kbps D-channel for singling between devices and the network and a 64 Kbps channel for synchronisation and monitoring. The total data rate of PRI is 2.048 Mbps. PRI is popularly referred to as '30B+D' because of the number of B-channels and D-channels, or I.421 because of the CCITT recommendation from which it is taken. This form of access is primarily intended for use in situations which require a large transmission capacity, such as when organisations make voice and data calls through an integrated services PBX.

Types of Interfaces

There are two types of ISDN interfaces (subscriber lines):

- Basic Rate Interface (BRI) – 2B+D
- Primary Rate Interface (PRI) – 23B+D

The difference between them is the number of channels available with one subscriber line. ISDN has also multiple channel within one physical line.

Copper wires are used for subscriber lines for BRI while optical fibres are used for PRI.

B-ISDN

The introduction of B-ISDN (Broadband ISDN), a next generation ISDN, is currently under study. As the name implies this type of ISDN enables high speed broad band transmission with user interface network speeds of 155 Mbits/s or 622 Mbits/s. B-ISDN also offers genuine TV and HDTV picture communication that is not possible with conventional ISDN.

B-ISDN is based on the ATM (Asynchronous Transfer Mode) that will be described later. Optical fibres are used for subscriber lines.

Frame Relay

Frame relay is a connection based service operating typically at 56Kbps or 1.5Mbps and can run to 100Mbps.

It has evolved from X.25 packet switching and the objective is to reduce network delays, protocol overheads and equipment cost. Error correction is done on an end to end basis rather than a link to link basis as in X.25 switching. Frame relay can support multiple users over the same line and can establish a permanent virtual circuit or a switched virtual circuit.

Advantages

- **High speed transmission.** This has been made possible by simplifying the X.25 protocol.
- **Multiplex transmission.** As with X.25 network, multiple channels can be provided on a single physical line for simultaneous communication with multiple parties.

Disadvantages

- **Frame discarded in case of network congestion.** If congestion occurs in the network, frame in the form of data is discarded within the network without transmission of this frame. The user must perform retransmission control as his own responsibility.

Switched Multi-megabit Data Service (SMDS)

SMDS is a connectionless broadband data service. Any SMDS station can send a frame to any other station on the same SMDS cloud. It operates typically at 1.5Mbps to 100Mbps. SMDS provides a switched connectionless data service at speeds of 34 Mbps for connection of LANs. SMDS packets are transported in the public network using the Distributed Queue Dual Bus (DQDB) IEE 802.6 standard, which uses packets fixed at 53 bytes. There is some overhead from this conversion process which reduces the bandwidth available to users to about 75% of the line speed. There are many access classes that limit the sustained data rate and burst data rate that can be injected into the network by a user. These access restrictions may result in discard of packets that exceed a certain limit. SMDS does not support timing. The higher speeds of SMDS will be of benefit to multimedia applications seeking to transfer large volumes of data quickly, but the lack of a time structure will reduce the obtainable video conferencing quality.

Asynchronous Transfer Mode (ATM)

The purpose of ATM is to provide high speed, low delay multiplexing and switching networks to support any type of user traffic, such as voice, data or video applications. This is specifically designed as a single technology for voice, video and data. ATM segments and multiplexes use traffic into small, fixed length units called cells to reduce and control delay. ATM can support different speeds, traffic types and quality of service matched to applications. ATM cells coming from a user are guaranteed delivery at the other end with a high probability and low delay. The cell is 53 octets, with 5 octets reserved for the cell header. ATM users have a dedicated connection to a high speed ATM switch. Each cell is identified with virtual circuit identifiers contained in the cell header. The ATM network uses these identifiers to relay the traffic through high speed ATM switches. Control of the priorities of packets in ATM switches enables guaranteed delivery of information.

ATM provides no error detection operations on users payload inside the cell. It provides no retransmission services and few operations are performed on the small header. The purpose of this approach is to implement a network fast enough to support multi megabit transfer rates.

Each ATM end point in a network has an ATM address associated with it to support dynamic connection establishment via signalling. These addresses are hierarchical in structure and globally unique. As a result, these addresses are routed. This allows ATM networks to eventually support a large number of ATM endpoints once a routing architecture and protocols to support it become available.

Advantages

- **High speed transmission.** This can be attained through the use of ATM transmission technology.
- **Multiplex transmission.** As in X.25 and frame relay network, multiple channels can be set within one physical line and communication is possible with multiple parties simultaneously.

Disadvantages

- **Cell discarding occurs with congestion.** When congestion occurs in the network, the cells in the form of data within the network are discarded and retransmission control cannot be carried out within the network. The user must be responsible for carrying out retransmission control with the other party.

Review Questions

1. What is network? How can it be helpful in providing multimedia services?
2. Explain different transmission media and also provide a comparative study of all with respect to multimedia applications.
3. Explain different types of WAN technologies.

4. What is the basic building block to make a WAN? Illustrate with the help of diagram.
5. What are different LAN topologies?
6. Why is layer structure recommended as a standard for network?
7. Explain ATM's usefulness in multimedia applications.
8. Explain SMDS.
9. Explain Frame relay.
10. Explain BRI and PRI with respect to ISDN.

CHAPTER VIII

Multimedia Platforms

1. *Introduction*...147
2. *De facto multimedia platform standards*...........148
3. *The Interactive Multimedia Association (IMA)*...149
4. *Multimedia Hardware*...................................... 150
5. *Systems Software*...156
6 *Emerging Trends*...159

CHAPTER 8

Multimedia Platforms

Introduction

There is a need to identify compatible hardware components that will provide the desired results on a desktop computer. The basic multimedia platform should be able to handle text, graphics, animation, photographs, full motion video, music, speech and other sounds. These elements, in the form of objects, may have to be integrated and manipulated in various combinations as individual screens. Such interactive programmes should present smooth sequences with image quality acceptable at least to the specific target audience of intended end users.

The PC can provide support to text and simple graphics, which could be accessed via menu driven interface. Apple and Commodore are considered to be the pioneer in launching multimedia systems during mid eighties. From it's first appearance, the Apple Macintosh proved to be a major influence on the personal computer market. It popularised the Graphical User Interface (GUI) and supported text, graphics, animation and sound output. It may be considered as the first multimedia personal computer. The Amiga of Commodore has also supported most of the things that are seen as multimedia today. Its features included two audio channels, speech synthesis, animation at 30 frames per second and video output compatible with the US television standards, all supported by a multitasking operating system.

These systems were readily adopted for applications such as videographics, presentations, interactive displays and Computer Based Training (CBT) systems. However, they had certain disadvantages for general business use, most notably their nonconformance with the *de facto* standards that had emerged for personal computing. These were based on Intel's 80x86 family of processors, the IBM PC bus architecture and the MS-DOS operating system.

De Facto Multimedia Platform Standards

Several desktop platforms exist on which multimedia presentations, interfaces and other applications can be implemented. These platforms not only use different operating systems but also employ different technologies for handling motion videos on their desktops.

This category includes Apple Macintosh, Commodore Amiga, Philips CD-I, Intel's DVI, IBM DOS based videodisk systems, NeXT computers and Windows/CD-ROM environments. Such platforms are incompatible with each other and a multimedia application developed on one cannot be played on another. Audio and video files are particularly sensitive in this respect and often can not run on any system other than the one on which they were authored.

Analogue video signals from laserdisks or VCRs as video sources are simply passed through and the desktop screen is used to display images. This method offers excellent quality because there is no conversion to digital format, but it does not allow any manipulation of the video within the multimedia system itself.

The video is digitised by employing necessary hardware solutions that implement the JPEG or MPEG or other compression schemes. For example, the Intel i750 chip, which forms the core of a video processor that handles compression, decompression, image manipulation and playback. The video is brought into the desktop through software techniques.

The Interactive Multimedia Association (IMA)

Due to incompatibility amongst different multimedia systems, suppliers of multimedia, hardware and software formed the IMA, an umbrella organisation whose goal is to agree on hardware and software specifications so that these will be acceptable to all in the multimedia business. Its main focus is the compatibility project, which consist of technical working groups dealing with the multimedia platform architectures, digital audio, digital video and data exchange issues.

Originally the IMA compatibility project conceived an agreement on the existence of several classes of multimedia platforms for which common standards could be accepted. IMA now emphasises the need to develop applications that are compatible with multiple multimedia platforms and is looking towards independent software developers to take the lead in solving the incompatibility problem. A Special Interest Group (SIG) of the IMA has supported the MPC (Multimedia Personal Computer) platform introduced by Microsoft.

IMA identified incompatible and inconsistent applications and enabling programme interfaces across all operating systems and hardware environments as the first major issue to be addressed. It deals with interactions of authoring systems and animation software with various operating systems and hardware devices. The second major issue is the data interchange problem, which involves sound, video and other files and their ability to run reliably on different platforms. Initial standards being worked upon along those lines concentrate on DOS, OS/2, Macintosh and Unix operating system platforms as the most numerous and significant to the development of interactive multimedia in business environments.

Multimedia Hardware

The basic IBM PC compatible machine was not a natural multimedia platform. It was weak on processing power and had required adaptor boards to provide integral support for audio or video. A whole industry of adaptor boards and related accessories grew up around the IBM PC and its clones. In the nineties, in order to open up the large installed base of PCs to multimedia applications, Microsoft announced a minimum configuration for a personal computer to run multimedia applications. The MPC platform standard announced by Microsoft is being supported by AT&T, CompuAdd, Creative Labs, Fujitsu, Headland Technology, Media Vision, NEC, Olivetti, Philips Consumer Electronics, Tandy, Video 7 and Zenith Data Systems. The MPC marketing Council, a subsidiary of the Software Publishers Association, was established to promote the specification and to issue licenses to products that conform to it. This council established the 16MHz 386SX minimum MPC standards. These are shown in Table 8.1.

Table 8.1 Minimum Configuration for MPC

Processor	16 MHz 386 SX
Memory	2MB
Hard disk	30 MB
Floppy disk	3.5" high density
Video display	640x480, 16 colours
Sound	8 bit digital sound, 8 note synthesizer, MIDI Playback
CD-ROM drive	150 KB/s sustained transfer rate, maximum average seek time 1 second
I/O devices	101 keyboard, two button mouse
Ports	MIDI I/O, joystick
Operating system	Windows 3.0 with multimedia extensions or Windows 3.1

IBM

IBM itself is providing an expanding range of multimedia machines, adaptors and software tools. During 1991 the company introduced a customised version of the IBM PS/2, under the brand name Ultimedia, the first model to have multimedia features as standard. The Ultimedia product range, which is expanding all the time, includes:

- A range of audio and video adaptors for capture and playback
- The PS/1, PS/2 and ValuePoint families of products and multimedia upgrade kits
- A desktop conferencing package called Person to Person, whose facilities include file transfer, shared whiteboard, remote pointer and optionally a video window
- A suite of kiosks, incorporating variations of the PS/2 and a touch screen, with optional transactional features (telephone and credit card reader)
- A Speech server series that analyses the spoken word

System software and a variety of software tools support these products. In addition, multimedia capabilities can be integrated into IBM's mainframes (ES/9000), mid range processors (AS/400) and personal workstations (RISC System 6000). In 1992, IBM announced a framework for distributed multimedia computing, which is closely aligned with the OSI reference model (IBM 1992). This document outlines the steps that IBM intends to take to provide both new systems, enabled with multimedia and enhancements to the traditional infrastructure, for distributed computing. It is likely to prove essential reading for managers who intend to introduce multimedia into a new or existing IBM environment.

The Macintosh Platform

Apple sees multimedia as an essential part of its present and future computing systems. Unlike IBM, it has made support for a range of data types and integral part of all its products since the mid 1980s.

All Macintoshes have built in speakers to play digitised sound in stereo and can support grey scale and colour images and animations. Several have support sound input or a built in microphone and a video port through which to play back presentations. Video capture and hardware assisted playback have been supported by boards from third party suppliers. The new range of Power Macs, based on Power PC processors, includes support for telephony, voice recognition, sound generation and improved handling of digital video.

Apple also sees CD-ROM as an important way to push the market forward and was one of the first companies to include an internal drive in its machines as a standard feature. A multimedia version of Performa 600, for example, includes a double speed multi session CD ROM drive that can play Photo CDs.

Key software products, which are bundled with the hardware, include Hypercard and an authoring tool that can be used to organise the information in a nonlinear way and QuickTime. The latter, described in more detail in section 8.5.3, provides software support for sound, video and animation (which Apple describes as dynamic data), software compression and decompression and standards for file formats and interfaces. Table 8.2 lists the minimum Macintosh Platform specifications.

Table 8.2 Macintosh Platform Specification

CPU	Macintosh II family (68030)
Memory	5 MB RAM
Storage	100 MB Hard Disk, 144 MB Floppy Disk, CD-ROM (Macintosh compatible)
Video	Apple RGB Monitors, Radius, RasterOps, SuperMac
Audio	Built-in sound capabilities, MIDI interfaces
Software	System 6.0 and 7.0, HyperCard, QuickTime

Intel's DVI Platform

DVI is a brand name for a set of i750 chips Intel developed to compress and decompress video for playback in realtime at the broadcast TV rate of 30 frames per second. These chips are programmable and facilitate the use of different compression techniques including JPEG and MPEG standards depending on the application. DVI compression schemes allow compression ratios upto 160:1., which means that up to 72 minutes of full screen full motion video and audio can be stored on a single CD-ROM. This can be played back in realtime at CD-ROM data rate of 150 Kbps because DVI can compress motion video down to 5Kb per frame. Manipulation of moving video and networking is also possible with this chip.

DVI technology was originally developed by the RCA Sarnoff Research Centre in Princeton, New Jersey, USA, which was sold to Intel after GE acquired RCA. IDVI products are available from Intel under the ActionMedia 750 label in the form of video capture and delivery boards, a full application development platform, development software and support services. DVI based products are also available from video board suppliers such as Fluent Machines and New Video Corporation for PCs and Macintosh respectively. Following table 8.3 shows the minimum DVI platform specifications.

Table 8.3 DVI Platform Specifications

CPU	25 MHz 386, 64 Mb Cache
Storage	4 Mb
Video	VGA monitor, ActionMedia 750 digitised board, ActionMedia 750 delivery board, 2 Mb VRAM module
Audio	14 bits sampling, Varying sampling rates
Software	DOS 4.0 or 5.0, Audio Video support system, OS/2 2.0 (or 1.3), Windows 3.x

Unix workstations

The Unix multimedia is a natural extension of many applications, such as document image processing, that currently run on this platform. These are particularly suitable for applications that combine advanced 2D and 3D graphics with multimedia data types.

- **Sun.** Sun is considered to be the first of the Unix workstation vendors to exploit the opportunity offered by multimedia. Audio I/O has been available on the SPARC station since its launch. Most of Sun's desktop systems currently support 16-bit audio I/O and a connection to the Integrated Services Digital Network (ISDN). A CD-ROM drive that supports the CD-ROM XA (Extended architecture) and photo CD specifications is available as an option. Support for still images, motion video and video communication is available in the form of adaptors from Sun and third party suppliers. The Sun Video capture/ compression card and video camera can be used with any SPARCstation. The systems run Solaris, Sun's operating system, which is based on Unix system V.4.

- **Silicon Graphics.** The Indy workstation of Silicon Graphics (SGI) provides hardware and software for capturing and communicating sound and image over a network or via an ISDN interface to a digital phone line. It comes with a small digital colour camera on top of the monitor, a microphone, internal speaker and stereo headphone. The Indy supports a wide range of I/O devices (including 3D stereo glasses) and can take analogue video from camcorder, video disk player or video camera. The audio subsystem supports four channel stereo input and output at 16 bit sampling rates. As with all SGI's systems, it offers high performance 2d and 3d graphics on the X window system. An ambitious user interface called Indigo Magic is designed to incorporate voice recognition so that the microphone can be used to control the workstation. Facilities for desktop conferencing such as call set up and shared whiteboard are supported by SGI's InPerson software.

The Amiga Platform

Commodore Amiga 1200/3000/4000 computers are designed to integrate computer and video technologies. It provides built in graphics, audio, realtime multitasking and advanced computer processing, which other systems can only achieve through a variety of add-on products. The Amiga 3000 platform is engineered to produce RGB analogue and digital video signals comparable with NTSC video signals of broadcast TV, VHS and video cameras. Add on products give the Amiga the capability to operate in MS-DOS, OS/2 and Macintosh environments and provide networking capabilities.

The Amiga platform is mainly used for design of business presentations and editing video, storyboarding and training applications. Commodore Dynamic Total Vision (CDTV) is another Amiga based interactive delivery platform whose CD-ROM drive plays CD-ROM titles, CD-audio, CD-graphics and CD MIDI data. It is designed to compete directly with CD-I products and computer game platform in the consumer markets. Table 8.5 shows minimum configuration.

Table 8.4 Minimum Amiga Platform Specifications

CPU	16 MHz 32 bit Motorola MC 68030
Memory	1 MB
Storage	40 MB Hard Drive, 1.22-MB Floppy Drive
Video	RGB Analogue and Digital Slots, VGA Monitor
Audio	Built-in Stereo Sound, Built-in English Text-to-Speech Device
Software	Amiga DOS 2.0, MS-DOS, OS/2 Bridging Software, Macintosh Bridging Software

The CD-I Platform

Philips developed the CD-I multimedia delivery platform in partnership with Sony and Matsushita, according to a standard known as the Green Book. CD-I is being positioned primarily as a consumer product based on the Motorola 68000 family processor and a proprietary realtime operating system. CD-I is a published specification.

CD-I allows integration of data, still graphics, audio and motion video on the same disk. However, full motion is only possible in windows at 15 fps and the quality of video is comparable to VHS. The CD 1910 CD-I platform announced by Philips plays all manufacturers' 3", 5", CD audio, Photo Cd, CD+Graphics and CD-I disks. Eventually, CD-I players will employ MPEG decompression chips.

The NeXT Multimedia Platform

The NeXT Cube workstation, with its roots in Macintosh technology, is based on 25 MHz Motorola 68040 processor with at least 8 MB of memory and built-in audio, video and CD-ROM. This offers Unix as an operating system and therefore capable for networking.

Systems Software

Microsoft Windows

Microsoft developed multimedia extensions for Windows in order to extend standard systems software including DOS and Windows to have greater integral multimedia capability. It is intended to provide a standard for multimedia much the same way as Windows does for GUI applications. A range of the following elements provides support for multimedia within Windows:

- Object Linking and Embedding (OLE) technology to let users insert multimedia elements into software programmes

- Media Command Interface (MCI) to allow Windows-compatible applications to control multimedia devices such as CD-ROM drives audio and animation players. The digital Video MCI command set, designed in conjunction with Intel, supports digital video computing

- Audio Video Interleaved (AVI), a file format for digital video under Windows, designed to be cross-platform compatible.

Microsoft's Visual Basic programming system also supports the use of multimedia data types including digital video, in applications. Visual Basic and Microsoft C++ will be adapted to target new platforms, providing a range of tools for both the linear and interactive video markets.

Video for Windows consists of a set of tools based on the AVI file format, together with an add on module for Windows 3.1 and a CD-ROM.

Intel and Microsoft created the Windows Telephony Application Programming Interface (TAPI) as a standard interface for the integration of telephones and personal computers.

The Multimedia Viewer is intended to meet the needs of multimedia publishers. Designed for use with an MPC or equivalent platform, it provides both authoring tools to enable publishers to create titles and runtime software to allow end users to play them back.

Multimedia Presentation Manager/2

IBM provides a multimedia version of its GUI, Presentation Manager to support Ultimedia hardware. This extends the OS/2 operating system to allow applications to control a wide variety of devices in a standardised manner. Features include:

- A common interface for the control of logical and physical devices.

- Services for reading, writing and manipulating multimedia data objects.

- Support for a variety of formats for image and audio files.

- Data streaming and synchronisation for the transfer of large amounts of data from one device to another.
- Close captioning to provide a visual representation of spoken words.
- A series of mini programmes called applets, each of which is designed to accomplish a single task such as playing an audio device.

The standard user interface conforms to IBM's Common User Access (CUA) specification. An optional toolkit contains sample programmes and documentation together with C language bindings to assist the developer.

QuickTime

Apple's QuickTime is open software architecture for Movie. The Movie is a term used by Apple that allows integration of dynamic data such as sound, video and animation. QuickTime applications supports cross-platform environment, such as QuickTime for Windows is the same as QuickTime 1.0 on the Macintosh.

It supports a two file format. The first is the Movie file format that contains dynamic data consisting of video and sound. The homogeneous data such as video or sound is grouped into tracks and gets synchronised when played back. The second format consists of extension to PICT, Apple's standard file format for graphic information and also supports any image compression scheme registered with the compression manager. Besides, previewing of small thumbnail versions of pictures makes it easier to browse still image libraries. There is a choice of three schemes for software compression and decompression of still images , animation and video.

Solaris Live

This is a new multimedia environment for Sun's workstations. This is a mixture of existing and new facilities that includes:

- An imaging library and APIs to support the capture, display, compression, decompression, transformation, storage and retrieval of video and image data.
- Libraries for 2D and 3D graphics applications.
- Driver interfaces for capturing, manipulating and playing 8 and 16 bit audio data streams.
- Tools to allow multimedia to be integrated into an application or sent over the network.
- Tools to support the capture and playback of image and video.

Emerging Trends

The above platforms for multimedia were designed for standalone applications. Multimedia information over local and wide area networks (LAN/WAN) are the need of hour. This information should be available on these networks in both stored and real time. New generations of products, which can support ad hoc communication between two or more people in the normal office environment, are coming into the market.

The PCs must have the following technical features to support realtime audio and video communication:

- They must support cameras and audio telephony equipment that have been the part of the traditional personal computer.
- They must be able to transmit realtime video and audio over LANs/WANs.
- They must be compatible with H.320 – the emerging international family of standards for audiovisual telephony.
- They must support data sharing and manipulation by two or more users.

They must also fit into the normal PC environment. For most business this is likely to be a combination of Intel 80x86 processors with MS Windows and a network operating system such as Novell NetWare.

Review Questions

1. What do you expect from the multimedia platform?

2. What are *de facto* multimedia platform standards?

3. What are different hardwares available in the market? Give a comparative study of all.

4. Who is the leader in the software market for multimedia?

5. Give a comparative study of all available softwares.

6. What are the future directions in the development of multimedia platforms?

CHAPTER IX

Multimedia and Internet

1. *Introduction..163*
2. *Components of the Internet...............................164*
3. *Multimedia and Internet Protocols...................170*
4. *Internet Protocols and ATM.............................178*
5. *ITU-T Standards..179*

CHAPTER 9

Multimedia and Internet

Introduction

The Internet is a computer network made up of thousands of networks worldwide. There is no one in charge of the Internet. There are organisations which develop technical aspects of this network, but no governing body is in control. Private companies own the Internet backbone through which Internet traffic flows. All computers on the Internet communicate with one another using the Transmission Control Protocol/Internet Protocol suite, abbreviated to TCP/IP. Computers on the Internet use client/server architecture. This means that the remote server machine provides files and services to the user's local client machine. Software can be installed on a client computer to take advantage of the latest access technology.

An Internet user has access to a wide variety of services namely electronic mail, file transfer, vast information resources, interest group membership, interactive collaboration, multimedia displays, real-time broadcasting, shopping opportunities and more. The Internet consists primarily of a variety of access protocols. Many of these protocols feature programmes that allow users to search for and retrieve material made available by the protocol.

Components of the Internet

World Wide Web (www)

The World Wide Web abbreviated as the Web, www, or W3 is a global system of hypertext and multimedia services. WWW is a client-server model that uses TCP/IP protocols. WWW consists of clients called browsers and servers called web servers. Web servers use http (HyperText Transmission protocol) and html (HyperText Markup Language) to make the www hypertext and multimedia services available to clients over the Internet. WWW supports hypertext to access several Internet protocols on a single interface. Hypertext or Hypermedia system allows interactive access to collections of documents. These documents can hold text (hypertext), graphics, sound, animations and video. These documents are linked together and may be seen as non distributed and distributed. In non-distributed, all documents are stored locally (like CD-ROM). In distributed, all documents are stored on remote servers.

Internet supports various protocols and network services. This includes e-mail, FTP, Gopher, Telnet, Usenet News. In addition to these, the world wide web has its own protocol.

The www provides a single interface for accessing all these protocols. This creates a convenient and user-friendly environment. It is no longer necessary to be conversant in these protocols. The web gathers together these protocols into a single system. Because of this feature and the web's ability to work with multimedia and advanced programmeming languages, the www is the fastest-growing component of the Internet.

The operation of the web relies primarily on hypertext. HyperText is a document that contains links (pointers) to other documents. A button represents these links. A single hypertext document can contain links to many documents. In the context of the web, button or graphics may serve as links to other documents, images, video and sound.

A page represents each document. The initial page for individual or organisation is called a home page. The page can contain many different types of information and must specify content, type of content, location and links. These pages are formatted with a mark up language called HTML (HyperText Markup Language) rather than fixed WYSIWYG (What You See Is What You Get) representation (e.g., word). With HTML, tags are placed within the text to accomplish document formatting, visual features such as font size, italics and bold and the creation of hypertext links. Graphics may also be incorporated into an HTML document. The HTML is an evolving language with new tags being added as each upgrade of the language is developed and released.

The web provides a vast array of experiences including multimedia presentations, real-time collaboration, interactive pages, radio and television broadcasts and the automatic push of information to a client computer. Newer programming languages such as Java and JavaScript are extending the capabilities of the web.

E-mail

Electronic mail, or e-mail, allows computer users, locally and worldwide, to exchange messages. E-mail users have an electronic mailbox into which incoming mail is dropped. Messages sent through e-mail can arrive within a matter of seconds. User accesses this mail with a mail reader programme, called Mail User Interface that is usually associated with computer account. One user may have different electronic mailboxes. Electronic mailbox is identified by an e-mail address and is given a user's account ID. This is not always true because on non-networked multi-user computer, e-mail address is just account ID.

Mail delivery among networked computers is more complicated. In this case, mail must identify computer as well as mailbox. Syntactically, e-mail address is composed of computer name and mailbox name, for example, user_id@domain.

E-mail message format contains header and body. Header includes delivery information and body carries message part. The header and body are separated by a blank line. An e-mail message can only be transmitted in form of 7-bit ASCII (American Standard Code for Information interchange) data. ASCII is a 7-bit code, resulting in a maximum of 128 characters. The data in e-mail could not contain arbitrary binary values e.g. executable programme. There are techniques for encoding binary data so that binary data may be transported.

A powerful aspect of e-mail is the option to send electronic files to a person's e-mail address. Non-ASCII files, known as binary files, may be attached to e-mail messages. These files are referred to as MIME (Multi-purpose Internet Mail Extensions) attachments. MIME extends and automates encoding mechanisms and was developed to help e-mail software handle a variety of file types. It allows inclusion of separate components, i.e., programmes, pictures, audio clips in a single mail message. The sending programme identifies the components so that the receiving programme can automatically extract and inform mail recipient. Many e-mail programmes, including Eudora and Netscape Messenger, offer the ability to read files written in HTML, which is itself of MIME type.

E-mail communication is really a two-part process. User composes mail with an e-mail interface programme. This mail transfer programme delivers mail to the destination and waits for mail to be placed in outgoing message queues. SMTP (Simple Mail Transfer Protocol) is standard application protocol for delivery of mail from source to destination. It provides reliable delivery of messages using TCP and message exchange between client and server including e-mail address lookup and e-mail address verification.

The e-mail can be looked into as an electronic version of paper based office memo, which is quick and much cheaper than a written communication. Because e-mail is encoded in an electronic medium, therefore fast, automatic processing in the form of sorting and reply are possible. It allows for quick, asynchronous communication across the entire Internet. Asynchronous communication consists of asynchronous characters with an output at a rate that is independently generated by the transmitter. The asynchronous characters are actually self-synchronised because they are framed by start and stop bits that delineate the character. E-mail is the most widely used Internet service world over. The best feature of the mail is its quick and reliable delivery of messages being contained in short data.

Telnet

A popular utility provided by TCP/IP is the TELNET. Telnet is a virtual terminal emulation facility that allows a user to connect to a remote system as if the user's terminal was hard wired to that remote system. This works on client server architecture. There is one Telnet server hosting various files and databases to share a client machine that accesses these resources. Telnet is a programme that allows logging into computers on the Internet and using online databases, library catalogues, chat services and more. The basic need to connect a Telnet to a computer is that its address should be known. This can consist of word (nic.gov.in) or numbers (140.147.254.3). The operation of this service is very simple. This requires just typing of the word telnet and then the address. Telnet is available on the www. Probably the most common web-based resources available through Telnet are library catalogues. A link to a telnet resource may look like any other link, but it will launch a telnet session to make the connection. A telnet programme must be installed on local computer and configured to web browser in order to work.

FTP (File Transfer Protocol)

The file transfer facilities are usually provided for by a mechanism known as the File Transfer Protocol (FTP). It is a simple featured file moving utility that allows a record oriented (one record at a time) transfer, a block transfer (which moves chunk of a file) or an image transfer. To transfer a file, the user invokes the host, FTP utility specifies file name, type (if necessary) remote destination.

This is both a programme and the method used to transfer files between computers on the Internet. Anonymous FTP is an option that allows users to transfer files from thousands of host computers on the Internet to their personal computer account. File transfer is quite rapid. FTP sites contain books, articles, software, games, images, sounds, multimedia, course work, data sets and more.

Archive

A computer site advertises and stores a large amount of public domain, shareware software and documentation. Archive functions as a catalogue of FTP sites. Archive is a programme that searches all the FTP sites on the Internet that are on its master list and stores the filenames in a central database. This database is available for users to search. When user contacts an archive site and enters a search string, archive searches the database and returns a list of all files that contain that string. The list provides with the address of the computer to contact and the directories where the files are stored.

Some archives are heavily used and therefore must be supported by multiple sites which are often located very far apart in this case. Each site should ideally have identical information available, therefore, they are mirrors of each other. When one site gets a new file, it must be mirrored to the other sites usually using FTP.

SMTP

It stands for Simple Mail Transfer Protocol. SMTP is a defined standard for e-mail over the TCP/IP protocol and therefore is widely used on the Internet. A utility that is somewhat popular provides a mechanism by which a user can specify a destination address, a particular path to follow (if desired) and a message. All e-mail servers use this protocol for message delivery and receipt.

E-mail Discussion Groups

One of the benefits of the Internet is the opportunity it offers to people worldwide to communicate via e-mail. The Internet is home to a large community of individuals who carry out active discussions organised around topic oriented forums distributed by e-mail. There are all kinds of discussion group like sports, space, politics, softwares, troubleshooting etc. Users port their queries in the form of e-mail and other's response to the query can be accessed over one discussion group.

Network Information Server

News, gopher and www are special servers for information which require a client software package to access. They can be thought of as network databases. WWW has been explained in section 9.2.1. Each server is powerful with some interconnectivity and requires a client application to allow the user to access the information. The main purpose of these client/servers is to help a user navigate the Internet to find information and files.

- **NEWS.** NEWS is made up of broad topics called news groups to which people can post or respond to posts. NEWS is available via Usenet, Internet and some commercial services. Almost nobody carries all the news groups. User access is through a news reader application that accesses a news server. There are many variations of newsreaders. Usenet News is a global electronic bulletin board system in which millions of computer users exchange information on a vast range of topics. There are thousands of Usenet newsgroups in existence. While many are academic in nature, numerous newsgroups are organised around recreational topics. Much serious computer related work takes place in Usenet discussions. A small number of e-mail discussion groups also exist as Usenet newsgroups.

- **Gopher.** Before the advent of the WWW, Gopher was the document access protocol of choice. Gopher is a menu utility mainly for text-based documents on the Internet, which simply uses FTP for retrieving files from archive sites. Gopher also uses a search utility called Veronica for aiding users in finding files in the gopher archive sites. Veronica can do keyword searches whereas Archie can only search for file names.

IRC, Chat and Instant Messaging

IRC is the Internet Relay Chat service in which participants around the world can "talk" to each other by typing in real time on hundreds of channels. These channels are usually based on a particular topic. To have access to IRC, an IRC software programme is essential. This programme connects user to an IRC server and allows him to visit IRC channels.

Chat programmes are now common on the web. They are sometimes included as a feature of a web site, where users can log into the chat room to exchange comments and information about the topics addressed on the site.

A variation of chat is the phenomenon of instant messaging. With instant messaging, a user on the web can contact another user currently logged in and type a conversation.

There are other services available on Internet like FAQ (Frequently Asked Questions), RFC (Request For Comments), FYI (For Your Information), MUD (Multi User Dimension) and WAIS (Wide Area Information Server).

MUDs are multi-user virtual reality games based on simulated worlds. Though traditionally text based, now graphical MUDs also exist. There are MUDs of all kinds on the Internet and many can be joined free of charge. MUDs are accessible by Telnet.

WAIS provides information lookup services to libraries and databases on the Internet. A simple WAIS client allows the user to select databases to search from a list. The user then provides keywords to search for and the WAIS client allows the user to view any matches found. This is cumbersome once the list of databases grows into the thousands. Screen-full after screen-full of database names scroll by one after another.

Multimedia and Internet Protocols

A protocol is basically a set of rules which governs transmission from one point to another. It is a software that is required to use the physical connection. It is responsible for establishing the connection, sending and receiving the data in packets. The software is called a protocol because there must be compatible software on each end but they do not have to be written by the same vendor. Instead a protocol for the proper exchange of data is defined and released as a standard (such as TCP-IP). As long as the vendor on each end adheres to the protocol, a connection can be sustained which will support an application.

The Internet is more of a phenomena than a network but is important when discussing multimedia because a popular Internet application, the www is capable of accessing and displaying multimedia formats such as pictures, audio and video. The current Internet has thrived and grown due to the existence of TCP implementations for a wide variety of classes of host computers. These various TCP implementations achieve robust interoperability. TCP is used for transmitting data from one computer to another by means of connection oriented methods. TCP is used for e-mail, FTP, Telnet, www and various other Internet services.

In early IP networks, a packet could be sent either to one receiver i.e. point to point or to all receivers i.e. broadcast. A single transmission, which could reach a specific group of receivers, was not possible. The idea of IP multicasting was developed to promote the audio and video transmissions in real-time through the Internet. The system of connected networks, which comprise the Internet, has also been used to carry live audio and video. Extensions to the TCP/IP protocols currently used have been proposed as Real Time Protocols (RTP). Broadcast of audio and video has taken place on the Multicast Backbone (MBONE), by allocating higher priority to audio and video information from within routers.

For many reasons, such as accounting, security and multimedia, it is desirable to treat different packets differently in the network. For example, multimedia is now on our desktop and will be an essential part of future networking. Multimedia applications need to acquire differing grades of network service, for voice, video, file transfer, etc. It is essential that this service information be propagated around the network. To support multimedia, features will be needed such as policy-based routing, flows, resource reservation, type of service and quality of service.

Primarily, followings are the various protocols:

TCP-IP

This stands for Transmission Control Protocol/ Internet Protocol. TCP/IP was developed by the United States Department Of Defence for it's ARPA (Advanced Research Project Agency) network. TCP-IP is a protocol that has been released as a standard which means that vendors can implement it independently and freely and yet it still works. Lots of free source code and the ability to use it royalty free make TCP/IP attractive to vendors. It has been implemented by a large number of different vendors and therefore is popular on the Internet.

TCP/IP is a four layer communication architecture as shown in fig. 9.1 that provides some reasonable network features such as end-to-end communications, unreliable communications, line fault handling, packet sequencing, inter-network routing and specialised function unique to Department of Defence communications needs such as standardised message priorities.

The bottom layer, network services, provides for communications to network hardware. The layer above the network services layer is referred to as the Internet Protocol (IP) layer. The IP layer is responsible for providing a datagram service that routes data packets between dissimilar network architecture (such as between Ethernet and, say X.25). IP does not guarantee the delivery of data. Data concurrency, sequencing and delivery guarantee is the job of the TCP protocol. TCP provides for error control, retransmission, packet sequencing and many other capabilities.

The Protocol of TCP/IP is as follows:

- **Internet Protocol (IP).** It provides a connectionless datagram network layer. Since networks vary in size, there are four different address formats or classes to consider:
  - **Class A.** addresses are for large networks with many devices
  - **Class B.** addresses are for medium-sized networks
  - **Class C.** addresses are for small networks (fewer than 256 devices)
  - **Class D.** addresses are multicast addresses

  The first few bits of each IP address indicate which of the address class formats it is using.

The address structures look like this:

- **Class A**

0	Network (7 bits)	Local address (24 bits)

- **Class B**

10	Network (14 bits)	Local address (16 bits)

- **Class C**

10	Network (14 bits)	Local address (16 bits)

- **Class D**

10	Network (14 bits)	Local address (16 bits)

◆ **ICMP.** It stands for Internet Control Message Protocol. It adds functionality to the IP protocol and can be considered as an extension to that protocol

◆ **UDP.** The User Datagram Protocol provides the rough equivalent of the ISO connectionless transport service

◆ **TCP.** The Transmission Control Protocol is a connection oriented reliable end-to-end transport protocol

The protocols which run above TCP include Telnet, a terminal access protocol and a file transfer protocol FTP, which have already been discussed.

Figure 9. 1 TCP/IP Communication Architecture

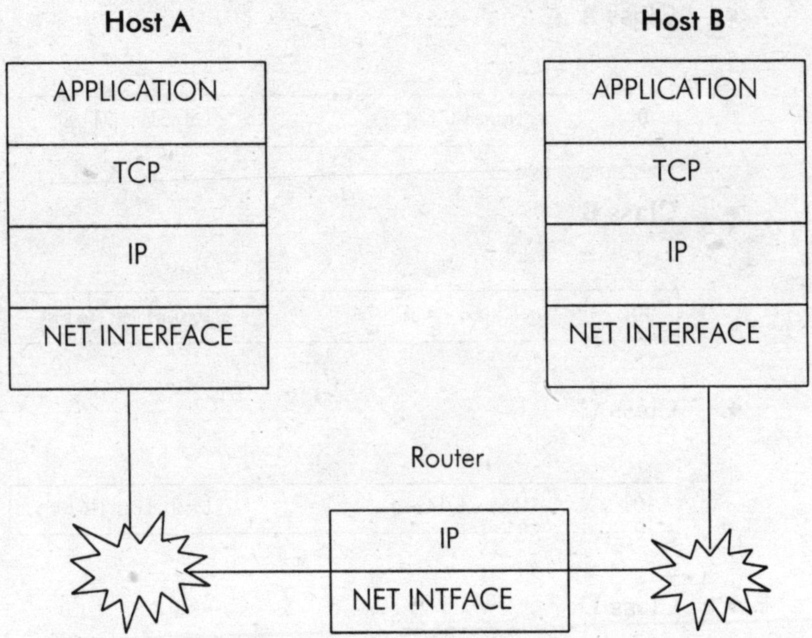

A successor to the current version of TCP/IP Version 4 is being discussed. While some motivation behind this is due to the need to increase the address space available, the opportunity is also being taken to review the need to increase the performance of Internet protocols for multimedia applications. The Internet Engineering Task Force (IETF) has resolved to move towards developing a replacement for the current TCP/IP Version 4 called IPng (IP next generation). This is discussed in next section. The delivery of digital video and audio programmes requires the capability to do broadcasting and selective multicasting efficiently. The interactive applications that the future cable networks will provide will be based on multimedia information streams that will have real time constraints. The largest fraction of the future broadband traffic will be due to real time voice and video streams. It will be necessary to provide performance bounds for bandwidth, jitter, latency and loss parametres, as well as synchronisation between media streams related by an application in a given session.

IPv6: The Future of IP

The current version of IP i.e. version 4 (IPv4) is about 20 years old. IPv4 has shown remarkable ability to move to new technologies. Internet Engineering Task Force (IETF), with consensus, has proposed entirely new version, IPv6, to address some specific problems. IPv6 is short for Internet Protocol, version 6. This emerging technology is also referred to as IPng (pronounced "I-Ping") which is short for Internet Protocol, next generation. IPv6 is a new system, currently under development, to be used for assigning Internet protocol addresses in the future.

An IP (Internet Protocol) address is a number that identifies a computer connected to the Internet. Every computer that is connected to the Internet must have a unique IP address. The motivation for change lies in the fact that currently, an IP address is a 32-bit addressing scheme. It consists of four sections separated by periods. Each section contains an 8-bit value represented as a number ranging from 0 to 255. This scheme allows for over a million networks. However, the allocation of these IP addresses follows a two level architecture that assigns IP numbers to a network and the hosts on that network. This architecture has proved to be an inefficient method for assigning IP address space and has led to the idea that the Internet will eventually run out of IP addresses. In this scheme most of the addresses lie in Class C and that is too small for many organisations. Class B network addresses are already almost exhausted.

The features of IPv6 scheme are that address size is 128 bits and header format will be entirely different from the IPv4. In this scheme, an IP address will consist of eight sections, each containing a 16-bit value. The number of IP addresses possible with this scheme is equal to the IPv4 address space squared, twice. The general syntax for the new IP addresses is to have the values of the IP address separated by colons, for example, 1080:0:0:0:8:800:200C: 417A. A major feature of IPv6 is that it will be fully compatible with the current IPv4 addressing system. The transition from the current IP addressing scheme to IPv6 is expected to take many years, but because the two systems are compatible, the transition is expected to be relatively smooth.

The advantage of IPv6 is not only in its large address space, but also in its flexible architecture. IPv6 is being designed to allow for future growth of networking technologies and expansion of the Internet. This will support audio and video and allow audio and video applications to establish appropriate connections. This is extensible and new features can be added more easily. With the use of multiple headers, efficiency and flexibility can also be increased.

Network media speeds are constantly increasing. It is essential that the Internet switching elements (routers) be able to keep up with the media speeds. A proper IPng router should be capable of routing IPng traffic over links at speeds that are capable of fully utilising an ATM switch on the link.

There are now many different LAN, MAN and WAN media, with individual link speeds ranging from a ones-of-bits per second to hundreds of gigabits per second. There will be multiple-access and point-to-point links on a switched and permanent basis. Switched circuits include both permanent connections such as X.25 and frame relay services and temporary types of dial up connections similar to today's SLIP and dial up PPP services and perhaps, ATM SVCs. Any IPng will need to operate over ATM. However, IPng still must be able to operate over other, more "traditional" network media. A host on an ATM network must be able to inter - operate with a host on another, non-ATM medium.

The Multicast Backbone (MBONE)

The Multicast Backbone (MBONE) provides a real time audio and video on the Internet. It is used for video and audio conferencing. The MBONE is being developed as a technology for low cost multimedia. Multicasting within MBONE enables multiple destinations to share the same information without replication. Internet routers and workstation software require some modifications to support multicasting. The MBONE is a virtual overlay network that uses the physical infrastructure of the existing Internet. Since not many routers in the Internet support multicasting, the MBONE is layered on top of the existing Internet protocols. In other words, a virtual network has been implemented over the IP network to bypass routers, which do not support multicasting and to enable some bandwidth to be reserved for multicasting. However audio and video on the MBONE must still compete with other traffic on parts of the network. This limits the quality of both the voice and video obtainable.

However current transport protocols exhibit some severe problems for high performance, especially for using hardware support. Existing protocols require a processing overhead, which takes longer than the transmission time on high speed networks. Networks that are connected to the MBONE must comply with special requirements for the available bandwidth. For video transmissions, a minimum bandwidth of 128 Kbps is required. Audio transmissions require a minimum of 9-16 Kbps.

Most of the MBONE tools use the User Datagram Protocol (UDP) instead of the usual Transport Control Protocol (TCP) because the reliability and flow control mechanisms of TCP are not practical for real-time broadcasting of multimedia data. The loss of an audio or video packet is acceptable rather than transmission delays because of TCP retransmissions. On top of UDP, most of the MBONE applications use the Real Time Transport Protocol (RTP). RTP has been explained in next section. Special purpose transport protocols have been developed. Some other examples are UDP (User Datagram Protocol), RDP (Reliable Datagram Protocol), NVP (Network Voice Protocol), PVP (Packet Video Protocol) and XTP (Xpress Transfer Protocol).

The Real Time Protocols (RTP) and The Real Time Control Protocol (RTCP)

The Real Time Transport Protocol (RTP) is used in real time applications such as video conferencing, audio broadcasting or Internet telephony and is usually implemented directly in those applications. Most of the MBONE tools use the RTP protocol for the delivery of real time data. Therefore, RTP is mostly used together with UDP. RTP itself is not aware of a connection. It operates over connection-oriented or connectionless lower layer protocols. Because RTP provides no reliability mechanisms and does not guarantee delivery, the application must decide if packet loss is acceptable or if it needs its own reliability routines. It also does not provide functions to ensure timely delivery or provide other quality-of-service guarantees. Real time services can be facilitated in an application by implementing following two protocols:

- Real Time Transport Protocol (RTP) is responsible for the transport of real time data packets that allow the synchronisation of multimedia data streaming from different applications.
- RTP Control Protocol (RTCP) controls and monitors the RTP session. The primary function of RTCP is to provide feedback about the quality of the RTP data distribution. This is comparable to the flow and congestion control functions of other transport protocols. Feedback from the receivers is necessary for diagnosing distribution faults. RTCP produces sender and receiver reports such as stream statistics and packet counts. It uses a separate UDP port from the RTP protocol.

Internet Protocols and ATM

An example of the issues in implementing this requirement is proposed IPng support for ATM. Current IP does not provide much support for a quality of service specification and provides no support for the specification of link level performance needs by an application directly. This is due to the fact that only a single type of link level performance is available with link technologies like Ethernet. As a result, all applications over IP receive the same level of link service.

ATM is a link level technology which provides the potential capability for applications at the TCP level to map to a single ATM virtual circuit for transport across an ATM network(s) customised to the network performance and traffic requirements for that application. The future Internet will be comprised of both conventional and "sophisticated" link technologies. The "sophisticated" features of link layers like ATM need to be incorporated into an Internet where data travels not only across an ATM network but also across several other existing LAN and WAN technologies. ATM allows for each logical channel to have a customisable set of performance and quality of service characteristics. Hence a single ATM link level media appears like an array of link level technologies each with customisable characteristics.

There are several parametres required to map ATM services from a higher level service like IPng [Brazdziunas94]. These ATM parametres can be categorised as: addressing parametres, connection QOS - related parametres, connection management information and ATM virtual circuit identifier. The first three categories provide support for ATM signalling. The last parametre, a connection identifier that maps IPng packets to ATM virtual circuits, provides support for an ATM virtual circuit per application when the end-to-end connection travels across an ATM subnetwork(s) (this does not assume that ATM is the only type of subnetwork that this connection travels across).

An ATM virtual circuit is established based upon a user's traffic characteristics and network performance objectives. These characteristics which include delay and throughput requirements can only be defined by the application level (at the transport level or above) as opposed to the inter-networking (IPng) level. For instance, a file transfer application transferring a 100 Mbyte file has very different link level performance requirements than a video application. The former requires a high throughput and low error rate connection whereas the latter requires a guaranteed bit rate. Applications will be responsible for reserving the required type of connection from the ATM link.

ITU-T Standards

The ITU-T is working on an I.374 standard network capabilities to support multimedia services. This will cover service control, connection management, service management and multimedia interaction for networks carrying multimedia traffic. Multimedia Application Programming Interfaces (APIs) will need to be able to interface to this standard.

Review Questions

1. Explain various components of an Internet.

2. Describe Internet protocols.

3. Describe few multimedia protocols.

4. How ATM can be useful in multimedia applications? Explain.

5. Explain the concept of E-mail.

6. What are Class A,B,C and D addresses?

CHAPTER X

Authoring System

1. *Introduction* *183*
2. *Authoring Paradigm* *184*
3. *Why Authoring Systems* *186*
4. *An Authoring System* *187*
5. *Desirable Features in an Authoring System* *188*
6. *Authoring Languages* *194*
7. *Conclusion* *195*

CHAPTER 10

Authoring System

Introduction

An Authoring System is a high level software tool which has pre-programmed software integration functions for the development of interactive multimedia software titles. Authoring systems vary widely in orientation, capabilities and learning curve. There is no such thing (at this time) as a completely point-and-click automated authoring system; some knowledge of heuristic thinking and algorithm design is necessary. Whether you realise it or not, authoring is actually just a speeded-up form of programming; you do not need to know the intricacies of a programming language. In developing an interactive multimedia application, the developer must be prepared to combine media elements such as text, graphics, animation, sound and video into a series of seamless sequences that may be randomly chosen for viewing and interaction by the ultimate end user of the application. Integration of the necessary hardware components creates the platforms that allow development and delivery of these applications. Software, however, is the most critical factor in manipulating and integration of multimedia content elements from various sources and successful operation of the system as a whole.

Authoring Paradigm

What is an authoring paradigm? It is also known as the authoring metaphor. This is the methodology by which the authoring system accomplishes its task. There are various paradigms, including scripting language, iconic/flow control, frame, card scripting, cast/score/scripting, hierarchical object, hypermedia linkage and tagging.

Scripting Language

The scripting language is the authoring method closest in form to traditional programming. This specifies (by filename) multimedia elements, sequencing, hotspots, synchronisation, etc. A powerful, object oriented scripting language is usually the centrepiece of such a system. The scripting language tends to be longer in development time (it takes longer time to code an individual interaction) but generally more powerful interactivity is possible. Since most scripting languages are interpreted instead of compiled, the runtime speed gains over other authoring methods are minimal.

Iconic/Flow Control

This tends to be the speediest (in development time) authoring system. It is best suited for rapid prototyping and short development time projects. The core of this system is the Icon Palette, containing the possible functions/interactions of a programme and the flow line, which shows the actual links between the icons. These programmes tend to be the slowest runtimes, because each interaction carries with it all of its possible permutations. The higher end packages, such as Authorware or IconAuthor, are extremely powerful and suffer least from runtime speed problems.

Frame

The frame paradigm is similar to the iconic/flow control paradigm in that it usually incorporates an icon palette. However, the links drawn between icons are conceptual and do not always represent the actual flow of the programme. This is a very fast development system but requires a good auto-debugging function, as it is visually undebuggable. The best of these have bundled compiled language scripting, such as Quest (whose scripting language is C) or Apple Media Kit.

Card/Scripting

The card/scripting paradigm provides a great deal of power (via the incorporated scripting language) but suffers from the index-card structure. It is excellently suited for hypertext applications and supremely suited for navigation intensive applications. Such programmes are easily extensible via XCMDs and DLLs. These are widely used for shareware applications. The best applications allow all objects (including individual graphic elements) to be scripted. Many entertainment applications are prototyped in a card/scripting system prior to compiled language coding.

Cast/Score/Scripting

The cast/score/scripting paradigm uses a music score as its primary authoring metaphor. The synchronous elements are shown in various horizontal "tracks" with simultaneity shown via the vertical columns. The true power of this metaphor lies in the ability to script the behaviour of each of the cast members. The most popular member of this paradigm is director, which is used in the creation of many commercial applications. These programmes are best suited for animation-intensive or synchronised media applications; they are easily extensible to handle other functions (such as hypertext) via XOBJs, XCMDs and DLLs.

Hierarchical Object

The hierarchical object paradigm uses an object metaphor (like OOP) which is visually represented by embedded objects and iconic properties. Although the learning curve is non-trivial, the visual representation of objects can make very complicated constructions possible.

Hypermedia Linkage

The hypermedia linkage paradigm is similar to the frame paradigm in a way that it shows conceptual links between elements; however, it lacks the frame paradigm's visual linkage metaphor.

Tagging Paradigm

Tagging paradigm uses tags in text files (for instance, SGML/HTML and WinHelp) to link pages, provide interactivity and integrate multimedia elements. They tend to have limited tracking capability and are best suited to online reference material like dictionaries and manuals.

Why Authoring Systems

Authoring systems are advantageous because they were designed with multimedia developers in mind. It generally takes about one eighth the time to develop an interactive multimedia project in an authoring system as opposed to programming it in compiled code. This means one eight the cost of programmer time and likely increased re-use of code (assuming that you pass this project's code to the next similar project and they use a similar or identical authoring system). However, the content creation (graphics, text, video, audio, animation, etc.) is not generally affected by the choice of an authoring system.

A single authoring system combines all the functions and interfaces required joining various media elements from different sources. This saves a significant amount of time and money for identification, design, testing and programming of such interfaces. Therefore, most authoring systems have object oriented tools within their own environment for development of complex interactive multimedia systems with relative ease even by individuals with no previous computer programming experience.

Authoring system vendors also recognise that content and format of multimedia applications are much more critical to success than just the capability to interactively process information and knowledge. They also differentiate the creators and developers and know that the former is much more important within the overall project effort. The vendors also know that such creators may not necessarily be familiar with computers or their operation and usage.

An Authoring System

An authoring system is basically a collection of integrated software routines and utilities with a very friendly GUI and built in facilities to automatically handle external inputs from analogue and digital sources. It's text handling options are similar to that of a publishing system and its graphics capabilities resemble those of a graphics presentation package. Animation is comparable to that found in typical animation programmes.

Unique to multimedia authoring systems are facilities to handle audio and video options in combination with the appropriate audio and video boards that add compression and speed to those inputs. Several functions for easy construction of interactivity, branching on a variety of conditions and extensive end user navigation are also built into authoring systems to relieve the developer from having to provide these numerous, repetitive tasks.

Desirable Features in an Authoring System

An authoring system generally contains a user friendly working interface, internal interfaces for accepting external media input sources, a facility to import text and graphics, draw and paint capabilities, animation features, audio and video manipulation and editing functions, various interactivity functions and a choice of user input controls. These major functional segments (given in the Table 10.1 breakdown into more than 60 specific features that are desirable in an authoring system, but almost no available products include all of these features. It is necessary to evaluate these products against the requirements of the application to determine which is likely to provide the best performance and most comprehensive coverage.

Table 10.1 Major Desirable Functions

Authoring Facility	Major Desirable Functions
User Interface	WYSIWIG, GUI, Icons, Integrated Flow Chart, Menus
External Input Interfaces	Video disk, VCR, CD-ROM, Digital Camera, Audio Cassette, Synthesised Audio Board, Video Digitiser, Full Motion Video Board, TV Tuner
Text Handling Options	ASCII Imports, Fonts,/Sizes/Colours/, Styles, Formats, Word Search, Paragraphs, High Screen Resolution
Graphic Options	Primitives, Freehand Drawing, Vector Based Drawing, Scaling and Rotation, Text Overlay, Cut and Paste, Fill, Clip Art, Palette Editing, Graphic Imports (PCX, Targa, TIFF, Windows Metafiles), Screen Capture
Animation Features	2-D, 3-D, Canned, Sprite, Cel, Path, Cycle, Tweening, Transitional Effects, External Animation
Audio Options	Computer Sounds, Analogue Sources, Digitised Sources, MIDI Interface, Digi-

Cont...

	tised Audio Board, Edit Digitised Audio, Speech Synthesis, Laser disk Audio Channels
Video Options	Full Screen Motion Video, Video Windows, Seamless Video disk Search, Multiple Video Inputs, Overlay Video with Text and Graphics
System Functions	Branching, Timeout, Notetaking, Bookmark, Calculator, Runtime Creation, Testing While Authoring, Graphical Database Maintenance, Navigational Buttons, Variables, Help, Printing, Documentation, External Links, Debugging/Editing Tools
End User Controls	Keyboard, Mouse, Touch-Screen, Graphic Tablet, Light Pen, Trackball, Joystick, Speech Recognition

A comprehensive authoring system is indeed a complex software product that usually requires several megabytes of storage and a relatively fast desktop platform to perform at peak efficiency.

The User Interface Design

- **WYSIWYG (What You See Is What You Get).** WYSIWVG, a valuable feature of any authoring facility, is a type of interface. This interface enables authors to work with screens that look exactly as users will see them. This reduces the necessity to code, test and modify and increases the author's productivity. In some authoring systems, however, it is necessary to code the application using descriptive commands and then switch to another screen.

- **GUI (Graphical User Interface).** A graphical interface is also desirable for facilitating communication with the developer and most authoring systems provide some form of GUI. Original Macintosh based products such as MacroMind Director and Authorware Professional were developed using the Apple GUI but similar concepts have been incorporated in other DOS based authoring systems such as IconAuthor, Authorware Professional for Windows, TIE and SAGE.

- **Icons.** This facilitates the development of the overall decision tree for an interactive multimedia application.

- **Integrated Flowchart.** The integrated flowchart is a dynamic document changing with the design of the application as it progresses.

- **Menus.** Menu driven working interfaces allow users to choose tools and objects for placement and linkage on each particular screen.

External Input Interfaces

- **Video disk, VCR, CD-ROM, Full Motion Video Board.** These are the most common external devices handled by authoring systems.

- **Scanner or Video Digitiser.** This device can handle graphic images and photographs.

- **Audio Inputs.** Interfaces to handle microphones, audiocassettes and synthesised audio are necessary for this activity.

Authoring systems such as Authorware Professional, Ask*Me Professional and Quest include interfaces for handling most of these devices.

Text Handling Options

- **Fonts/Sizes/Colours/Styles, Formatting, Word Search.** The good authoring system must include built-in text manipulating facilities that combine word processing and publishing capabilities. Availability of scalable fonts, choice of several styles, sizes and colours for text are basic requirements for design of any screen.

- **ASCII imports.** Authoring systems without extensive built-in text handling capabilities will stress on the ability to import ASCII and other publishing file formats.

Graphics Options

Authoring systems offer a combination of basic graphics, drawing, painting and import facilities but the number of specific features and quality of output varies greatly among authoring systems.

- **Primitive.** These are the rectangles, polygons, ellipses, arcs, wedges and bars that speed up development of graphic settings and images. Not all authoring systems offer these facilities.

- **Freehand drawing, cut and paste, colour palette editing.** Particularly all authoring systems provide these facilities but the quality of graphics created by these functions depends upon the maximum screen resolution supported by a particular product and the number of concurrent colours handled by the system.

- **Scaling and rotation, cut and paste, fill, text overlay.** Using these functions can enhance the usefulness of object. Some systems such as Quest, offer excellent paste capabilities that allow placement of shapes in front or behind other graphics on the screen

- **Clip art.** This may not be available with all authoring systems. This feature is not as critical since most designers prefer to create their own clips rather than use standard, universal symbols.

- **Graphic imports.** Even the best built-in graphics facility will not be sufficient to give an authoring system all the graphics capabilities available from specialised graphic packages, so the ability to import specific graphic files becomes important. Many authoring systems support PCX files but other graphic files are not widely supported. Although specific needs will vary, more popular graphic files such as TIFF, PICT, DIB, EPSF and Windows Metafile should be available for import

- **Screen capturing.** The systems that offer this feature may vary. Some systems capture screen to be used as captured while others offer editing facility. They may also vary in the procedure to capture the screen.

Animation Features

Animation of objects on multimedia screens is a very important function. It is difficult to visualise an application without it.

- **Path animation.** This is basic type of animation. One or more objects are made to move along a defined path along the screen. These objects can be 2-D or 3-D (CAD/CAM) in nature.
- **Cycle animation.** This involves a series of shapes or objects that are displayed in sequence at the same location. This type of animation can be used to simulate motion in machinery.
- **Transitional effects.** These are the special effects that add a lot of professional style to multimedia presentations as screen change. The number of such effects in an authoring system varies from none to several dozen. Table 10.2 shows a list of some popular useful transition effects.

Table 10.2 Transition Effects

Effect	Resulting Action
Draw	Draws a new frame into the screen from any side
Wipe	New frame pushes old out in any direction
Fade	Objects fade in with/without shimmering effect
Mosaic	Screen appears in form of random squares
Sweep	Frame appears like a radar sweep from centre or diagonally from chosen corners
Pull	Old frame is pulled off, up , down or sideways revealing new frame underneath
Expansion	Frame appears out of a point in centre screen
Contraction	Frame draws into a point from outside edges
Halving	Vertical/horizontal halves slide into opposition
Curtain	Frame opens or closes like a theatre curtain
Slither	Colours are removed from screen line by line

Audio Options

- **Digitizer audio boards.** The computer or digitized audio files created by digitizer audio boards can be played. Audio can add very much to a multimedia presentation at a much lower cost in hardware and storage than video. The quality of audio depends on the quality of the original source recording and the quality of the speakers installed with the application system.

- Many authoring systems provide facility to generate simple computer beeps in applications. These beeps could be reinforced with flashing colours and advisory messages.

- **Analogue sources and digitized sources.** Most authoring systems support analogue and digital audio source inputs and generates computer audio files with a sound editor programming facility.

- **Laser disk audio channels.** Most authoring systems treat laser disk audio channels separately. These provide additional flexibility for audio.

- **Speech synthesis.** Some applications may require synthetic speech and sounds.

- **MIDI.** It is not supported by many authoring systems although it will inevitably become more popular as a delivery platform for playing music.

Video Options

Motion video demands a tremendous overhead in storage and speed from a development platform. Therefore, the video options have become important. Basically, most authoring systems provide support for:

- Manipulating full screen and window based motion videos.

- Controlling the search for video segments on storage devices.

- Synchronising inputs from several video sources, including still frame images and associated sounds.

There are two sets of video commands. The first one is the command for integrating still frame or motion video objects with an application's text and graphics elements. The second command is for editing video frames within a storage device. Both are critical in development.

Authoring Languages

Authoring languages are a specific set of procedure and commands for creating CBT applications. It requires considerable programming skills and training to implement.

- TenCORE by Computer Teaching Corporation is one of the most widely used authoring language for this purpose.
- IMSATT-2000 is another object oriented authoring language based on FORTH, a lesser known AI (Artificial Intelligence) language.
- Some of the authoring systems offer authoring language modules as part of the package. QUEST, for example, includes a QAL (Quest Authoring Language) module.
- Following Table 10.3 shows some popularly known authoring systems with authoring language facility:

Table 10.3 Authoring Languages Facility

Authoring Systems	Associated Languages
CDS/Genesis	Basic, C, Pascal
Guide	LOGiiX
MacroMind Director	Lingo
QUEST	Pascal like QAL
TIE	Accord Tutor Code
ToolBook	Open Script

Existence of an authoring language provides additional flexibility to developers who are programmers and to create additional functions not covered by the authoring system itself.

Conclusion

Selection of an authoring system for development of an interactive multimedia system will depend on the following points:

- Flexibility of design
- Resource requirements
- Ease of development
- Ability to integrate project team successfully
- Time and cost of the undertaking.

Review Questions

1. Why does anyone want to use an authoring system?
2. Explain in brief the facilities offered by the multimedia system.
3. What is an authoring paradigm?
4. Explain animation features in an authoring system.
5. How will you select an authoring system?

CHAPTER XI

Authoring System

1. *Introduction* 199
2. *The Basics of Animation* 200
3. *Animation Principles* 202
4. *Tools* 203

CHAPTER 11

Animation

Introduction

Animation is the process of assigning time-varying geometry and behaviour to a modelled object. In other words, modelled objects are brought to life in animation. Although animation is considered synonymous with motion, it covers all changes that have a visual effect. It thus includes the time varying position, shape, colour, transparency, structure and texture of an object. It also involves changes in lighting, camera position, orientation and focus and even changes of rendering technique.

History of animation can be traced from the early 1800s to just before the advent of the personal computer. Advent of computers and its influence on the field of animation can be seen widely. It is widely used in the entertainment industry and is also being applied in education, in industrial applications such as control systems and heads up displays and flight simulators for aircraft and in scientific research.

The Basics of Animation

- **Shape.** This is perhaps most affected by an object's actual motion and it is easy to understand. Both shape and position are spatial features and when the object is put in motion as a whole, it is only natural to expect that parts of its contour will, to some extent, displace relative to each other. When this is neglected in computer animation, the resulting 3D motion may seem flat, rigid, mechanistic.

- **Colour and Texture.** Real world objects rarely (if ever) exhibit any significant changes in the hue component of their visible colour. However, during motion, they can vary the brightness and, to a lesser extent, saturation because of varying lighting conditions along the motion path. Imitating this effect is perhaps the effective method to turn a monotonous linear motion into an eye catcher.

- **Persistence of Vision: The Illusion of Movement.** The human visual system is designed with what is called persistence of vision. In persistent of vision there is always an illusion of the visual field in front of the eyes for a short period even after blinking. This mechanism varies with different conditions but is generally clocked at from 1/10 to 1/5 of a second. Film takes advantage of persistence of vision by providing limited samples of live action movement, letting the mind fill in the gaps for a sense of smooth motion. Animation mimics live action footage by changing images quickly enough to also take advantage of persistence of vision, also giving the illusion of movement. This is very important. If images change too slowly, they will no longer appear to move. Below a certain threshold (which varies somewhat with the conditions of the image), the illusion of motion stops and there will be only a slide show. Media vary in how many images they have per second. 8mm and Super 8mm have 18 frames of film per second (fps). Larger film stocks (16mm, 35mm, etc.) generally run at 24 fps.

- **Perception of Motion is Logarithmic, not Linear.** A second principle of animation, based again on human perception, is the fact that making a series of movements equidistant will not make it appear smooth to the eye. When distances are plotted logarithmically, they appear smooth to the viewer. This business of logarithmic movement holds for everything from a character lifting his arm to a zoom-in or zoom-out.

Non-linearity in animation is not as geometrically simple a concept as it sounds. In mathematical terms, non-linearity means that the derivatives of the second, third and higher orders form some variable. This may be an object's size, spatial coordinate, character of motion or any other aspect. To find an analogue for this animation concept, consider this fact from the science of acoustics. A sound containing only a first order sinusoid, without any overtones (harmonics), is very sharp, shallow, mechanistic. To get a rich, lively sound of an interesting timbre, you should add some higher order components to it. Analogously, to make a motion interesting, you should expand its linear base by some nonlinear components of gradual unfolding, growth, or inflexion.

- **Trajectories and Key Drawings.** A trajectory is the path of motion being planned to use. The key drawings are the high points of the movements, or the most telling poses. Classic, naturalistic style animation has the drawings between key drawings at roughly logarithmic intervals: this is known as "ease-in" and "ease-out". Character animation (people and animals) relies mainly on key drawings. Animation of objects and effects depends more on trajectories. This can become quite time-consuming with multiple objects, as each object needs its own trajectory worked out.

- **Emphasising Movement for a Livelier Effect.** Classic animation uses several tricks to make movement snappier and more emphatic and take away a certain tapioca-like sameness of straight, flat-footed animation. Exaggerated, comic animation goes wild with these things; naturalistic animation uses them with more restraint. It's all a matter of style. Not all styles of animation use these things, but this is a little bag of tricks that is handy to have.

Animation Principles

There are a number of the following general principles:

- **Natural inherent motions.** Follow the natural inherent motions for any objects being animated. However, natural motion is a bit more abstract concept; it is not as simple as apples always dropping down and balloons always ascending. Finding an engaging natural motion for an object may involve analysing many of its aspects, including its inherent static dynamism, architectonics, common patterns of perception, etc.

- **Non Linear animation.** This is explained in last section also. By eliminating linearity, monotony in motion may be avoided. Although a static straight line has a certain aesthetic appeal due to its geometric perfection, a monotone linear motion is much less likely to work satisfactorily.

- **Accelerate or decelerate.** This is also a part of nonlinear animation. All instances of motion must be accelerated or decelerated. Constant speed adds a mechanic feeling to any movement.

- Use **curvilinear motion paths** instead of linear ones where possible, even if the curve is a simple circle. When moving an object along a linear path, rotating it at some degree during the shift will help to enliven it. Using rotation in combination with acceleration or deceleration will make a motion much more organic.

- Adding a third dimension to your motion may compensate for its too linear character. Only a simple trick of enlarging or reducing an object dynamically gives it an impression of "emerging" or "sinking" relative to the plane of the screen. Again, this technique can be used in combination with linear motion, accelerating/decelerating and rotation.

- Colour and texture effects can, to some extent, mask the linearity of a motion. Combined with a gradual darkening/lightening, transparency variation, or a moving highlight even an absolutely monotonous progression may turn into an interesting experience.

- Similarly, about any transformation of an object, such as shape morphing or tweening forces us to watch it with much closer attention, even if the object is immobile or involved in a simple linear motion. Transformations are something computers can do amazingly well and creative opportunities are enormous.
- With linear motions, try, at the very least, to make them as short as possible. Avoid frustrating the viewer by pushing an object too far in a too monotonous manner. For short bits of motion, it is much more difficult for the eye to notice their linearity.

Tools

Computer animation can be done on a different type of computer. Simple cell animation requires nothing more than a computer system capable of simple graphics with proper animation software. Unfortunately, most of the computer animations that are shown on television and in other areas are done on extremely sophisticated workstations. This section is broken into two sections, software and hardware. In the hardware section, all the different computer platforms on which computer animation is done are explained. The software is explained in the software section. Only the most popular and most well known software is explained, since it would be practically impossible to name all computer animation programmes because there are so many of them.

Hardware

Hardware comes in many shapes, sizes and capabilities. Some hardware is specialised to do only certain tasks. Other kinds of hardware do other things. The following is the most common hardware used in the field of computer animation:

- **SGI.** The SGI platform is one of the most widely used hardware platforms in professional or broadcast quality computer animation productions. SGI stands for Silicon Graphics Inc. SGI computers are extremely fast, produce excellent results and operate using the widespread UNIX operating system. SIGs are produced by Silicon Graphics.

- **PC's.** PC's are very versatile machines. They have been around for years and are favourites of many computer users. Because of their combination of flexibility and power, PC's have proven to be very useful for small companies and other businesses as platforms to do computer animation. Applications such as 3D Studio and Animator Studio are used on PC's to make animations. PC's are relatively cheap and provide pretty good quality. Recently though, PC's have been getting a lot of attention from different production houses because of their relatively small price and the quality of the finished products.

- **Macintosh.** Macintosh (Macs) were originally designed to be graphic and desktop publishing machines. Macs did not become that widely known until recently, when newer and faster models came out. Many people consider Macs slow and inefficient but that is not necessarily true. Right now with the advent of the Power Macintosh, the Mac is a pretty useful tool for smallscale companies wishing to do nice looking applications. Many companies are producing computer graphics and animation software for the Macintosh. Some of these are Abode with products such as PhotoShop and Premiere and Strata with Strata Studio Pro.

- **Amiga.** Originally owned by Commodore, Amiga computers have held their position in the computer animation industry for a number of years. There are two software packages that Amigas are basically known for: Video Toaster and LightWave 3D. The Amiga is based on a Commodore but it has been greatly customised to be a graphics machine. Many television shows use Amiga's for their special effects and animations.

Software

There are literally hundreds of computer animation and graphics software packages out there, however, only a few are considered industry favourites. The software mentioned here are only the tip of the iceberg. These are some of the most popular software packages used by companies, schools and individuals all around the globe.

- **3DStudio Max.** This is a successor to 3DStudio 3.0. 3DStudio Max runs under Windows NT. It is entirely object oriented, featuring new improvements such as volumetric lighting, space wraps and an all new redesigned interface.

- **3Dstudio.** 3DStudio is a 3D computer graphics programme and runs on PCs. It is relatively easy to use. Many schools and small time production studios use 3DStudio to satisfy their needs. 3DStudio is created by AutoDesk. 3DStudio consists of a 2D modeler in which shapes can be drawn, a 3D Lofter, in which 2D shapes can be extruded, twisted, or solidified to create 3D objects.

- **LightWave3D.** LightWave 3D is another high end PC 3D-computer graphics software package. Originally developed for the Amiga platform, LightWave 3D is now also available on the PC. It is used in quite a few television productions such as Babylon 5 and SeaQuest.

- **Adobe PhotoShop.** Although Adobe PhotoShop is not a computer animation application, it is one of the top of the line graphics programmes. It is created by Abode. PhotoShop runs both on Macs and PC, Windows and even on SGI. It can be used to touch up digitized images or to create graphics from scratch.

- **Adobe Premiere.** Adobe Premier, just like the name says, is created by Abode. It is a tool used to composite digitised video, stills and apply a variety of transitions and special effects. Adobe Premiere runs both on Macintoshes and PC Windows.

- **AliasIWavefront.** Alias was produced by the company that used to be Alias, but now has joined with Wavefront and is known as AliasIWavefront. It runs on SGI. Alias is well known for its great modeler which is capable of modeling some have the most complicated objects. Also, this software package is very flexible, allowing for programmers to create software that will run hand in hand with Alias.

- **Animator Studio.** Animator Studio is a cell animation programme from AutoDesk. Its predecessor was Animator Pro for PC DOS. Animator Studio runs under Windows. It has a multitude of features that minimise the animation creation time.

- **Elastic Reality.** Elastic Reality is one of the top of the line morphing programmes and runs on Macs and SGI. One of the great features of Elastic Reality as opposed to other programmes is that it uses lines as opposed to points to define the morphing area. Elastic Reality also allows to morph video as well as still images.

- **Soft Image.** One of the three top most computer animation software packages. Soft Image is used in many top production studios around the country and around the world.

- **Strata Studio Pro** Strata Studio Pro is probably the most will known 3D graphics application on the Macintosh. It is created by Strata Inc. Strata Studio Pro is mainly a still graphic rendering application, but it does have animation capabilities. Graphics for some games such as Myst were created in Strata Studio Pro.

Review Questions

1. What is animation? Is it recent development or not? Explain.

2. What is persistence of vision? Explain illusion of motion.

3. Perception of motion in logarithmic. Explain.

4. What are animation principles?

5. Explain computer animation tools.